Transgender Explained For Those Who Are Not

Joanne Herman

author**HOUSE**®

AuthorHouse™
1663 Liberty Drive
Bloomington, IN 47403
www.authorhouse.com
Phone: 1-800-839-8640

Cover photo by Mark Ostow Photography

First published by AuthorHouse   9/29/2009

ISBN: 978-1-4490-2966-1 (e)
ISBN: 978-1-4490-2957-9 (sc)

Library of Congress Control Number: 2009909612

Printed in the United States of America
Bloomington, Indiana

This book is printed on acid-free paper.

For the never-ending understanding
and forgiveness of my family.

I promised them I would just blend in, but it was
just too compelling to do whatever I could to make it
easier for those coming along behind me.

Contents

Acknowledgments

I owe a great debt of gratitude to the New England Foundation for the Arts (NEFA) and especially to my manager, Laura Paul. I came to Laura in 2002 after my employer made it clear that I could not stay after I transitioned to live as a female later that year. I had heard that Laura had an opening for a Financial Controller. It would be a step down from the Director of Finance position I held at the time, but I was determined that I was not going to become another transgender statistic: I did not want to be fired from my current job and unable to find another.

I had done some accounting consulting for NEFA, so she knew my work and was excited about my interest. But she almost fell off her chair when I told her about my transition plans. She had seen no clue! Yet when she regained composure, she just smiled and said, "That shouldn't affect your ability to do the job, should it?" She quickly organized a meeting with Executive Director Sam Miller and Deputy Director Rebecca Blunk (who has now become executive director). A few weeks later, I excitedly opened a NEFA envelope to find a job offer addressed to me as Joanne, specifying a start date right after my transition to female.

We chose to inform NEFA's employees about my past before I started employment, knowing that I might be a little awkward in my first months as a woman after years of being socialized as a male. I am now approaching my seventh anniversary at NEFA, and I am enormously grateful that the staff has never once treated me as anything other than just another woman in the office.

I am, though, most grateful to Laura. I have done good work at NEFA—of that I am certain—but what she has given me in return (aside from the modest compensation of a non-profit, of course) has been priceless. She has gently coached and mentored me in my new life as a woman. She has always been a willing ear for venting about the latest personal difficultly I faced or effusing about the latest personal triumph I achieved. She has demonstrated a confidence in me that has never waivered since the day of my interview. And, in the process, her support has allowed me to blossom as Joanne far beyond anything I could have imagined. I will never be able to repay Laura for this.

I am also grateful to Old South Church in Boston (United Church of Christ), Rev. Nancy Taylor, Rev. Quinn Caldwell, and Rev. Jennifer Mills-Knutsen for being there for me at another critical point in my life. You can read all about this in the chapter "My Faith Story." I have always felt welcomed at Old South as a transgender person, and I feel proud to be part of a congregation that does Christianity right.

I am indebted to Simon Aronoff for editing the columns I wrote for Advocate.com, which are the basis for much of this book. I'm glad that Simon always nudged me to word things in a way that included those whose transgender experience has differed from mine. I also thank Mara Keisling, Executive Director of the National Center for Transgender Equality, for her early support and promotion of my work, which included letting Simon do his editing for me while he was on NCTE time. Mara and her organization have done so much for the transgender community, and we all owe her a huge thank you.

I thank Bruce Steele, former Publisher of *The Advocate,* for taking a chance on an unknown transgender writer named Joanne Herman that grew into the thirteen-column Transgender 101 series. I thank Cathy Renna of Renna Communications and Carisa Cunningham of GLAD (the Boston-based LGBT advocacy and legal group, not to be confused with the LGBT national media watchdog GLAAD) for encouraging Bruce to take that chance. I also thank Bruce's successor, Anne Stockwell, for signing me up for a subsequent eight columns on advanced transgender issues. I know these columns have helped many.

Profound thanks go to Prof. Lynn Conway for her groundbreaking work on prevalence and for helping me summarize her findings into the chapter of that name. Lynn's Web site has been an invaluable source of information, encouragement, and strength to a transgender community whose members previously suffered greatly from information isolation.

I give a big thank you to Jennifer Levi, Director of GLAD's Transgender Rights Project. As one of the country's top attorneys in the emerging field of transgender law, Jennifer's schedule is always full, and yet she has always made time for me whenever I needed the legal perspective on a topic.

For my good friend Linda Markin, I reserve the warmest of hugs. Linda and I met at Dartmouth's second LGBT all-class reunion in 2004, and since then Linda has been a constant source of understanding, wisdom and compassion in my integration into my new gender.

Finally, I am indebted to Brian McNaught, the man the *New York Times* called "the godfather of gay diversity training," for lending his wisdom and encouragement to my work, and for patiently guiding me through the process of publishing my first book.

Foreword

Each time I am in front of an audience of senior executives whose company has a policy prohibiting discrimination based upon gender identity and expression, I ask, "Who feels comfortable explaining to others what 'transgender' means?" No one raises his or her hand. There is, in fact, usually a clear look of fear.

"Just because we can't explain it," argued the head of one firm's legal department, "doesn't mean that we'll discriminate."

"No," I replied, "but it does mean that it would be very difficult for a transgender person to identify him or herself in an atmosphere of ignorance. To create a safe and productive work environment for transgender people, we need to put a face on the issue for managers and other employees before a colleague confronts us with their need for understanding."

Joanne Herman provides a wonderful face and a very useful understanding of the various components of the transgender spectrum in this well-written and easy-to-understand primer. While no one individual's personal experience speaks for those of all transgender people, as she is eager to point out, she is an excellent educator on the basic language and personal nuances of the topic, as well as a great storyteller.

It's my experience as a corporate diversity trainer and sexuality educator, as well as that of a gay male raised in a large Irish Catholic Midwestern family, that ignorance is the parent of fear, and fear is the parent of hatred. Many of us, who have had the experience of traveling to a foreign country in which we didn't know the language, recognize the anxiety that can come from being plunged into the unknown. Our fear of making a mistake or of being taken advantage of can prompt feelings of anger and resentment. The subject of "transgender" is a foreign country in which most people don't know the language. Despite the advances we have witnessed in legal protection of transgender people around the world, many of us are still fumbling anxiously because we're consciously incompetent with the topic.

In getting past our discomfort with the unknown, there is nothing more effective in lowering anxiety than having a personal encounter with someone who comes from the world we fear. That has certainly been my experience in life, particularly with transgender issues. Hearing the personal stories of men and women on the transgender continuum who first experienced true happiness when they had the courage to self-identify and embrace themselves enabled me to get past my ignorance-based fears. Joanne Herman was one of my cherished teachers. I'm delighted that she has become one of yours too.

Brian McNaught

Corporate diversity consultant and award-winning author

Introduction

"You are so good at explaining this, you should write a book."

I have heard this from many people. While I always appreciated the compliment, I wondered how it was that these kind folks had never understood what transgender was all about. After all, hadn't they heard the stories of famous transgender people?

For those of my parent's generation: Christine Jorgensen, or

For those of my generation: Renée Richards or Jan Morris, or

For those of my stepdaughters' generation: Alexis Arquette or Chaz Bono?

Hadn't they seen on Oprah transgender writers such as Jennifer Finney Boylan, author of *She's Not There: A Life in Two Genders,* a bestselling memoir now in its eighth printing and available in many languages?

Or hadn't they read one of the other memoirs by transgender authors or perhaps encountered the subject in psychology or sociology texts while in college?

"No, really, you need to write a book!"

What all of these folks have had in common was that they were parents, relatives, colleagues, or friends who had a transgender person in their lives for the first time. In some cases, the people were journalists on a deadline to finish a story about a transgender person in their area.

What they seem to have appreciated was my short, logical, and non-technical explanation to almost any question they threw at me. They did not have time to read an entire book on the subject; they needed a quick, topical reference written in language they could easily understand.

I hope this book can be that reference.

This book assembles by topic updated versions of the numerous articles I wrote for Advocate.com in 2006–2007 and includes a few new ones. Together, they cover all of the key areas, from the basics to success stories and gender transition regret. Each one can be read independently, but together they will give you a complete understanding of the basic aspects of being transgender.

What qualifies me to write about the subject? I am a transgender woman, true, but I do not have a background in psychiatry or sociology. Actually, you'll be hard-pressed to find a transgender person in academia who does. Until the World Wide Web became widely accessible in the 1990s, society tended to regard transgender people as animals who were unable to speak for themselves and who were so misguided that only a non-transgender expert could possibly be credible. This belief effectively prevented transgender people from gaining jobs in psychiatry, psychology, and sociology and thereby prevented any serious challenge to the stigmatizing bias these experts have tended to espouse.

The Web has had a big impact on this situation. Transgender people, who previously felt isolated and alone, have been able to connect with each other. This connection has not only served to validate our individual beliefs of being transgender, it has also empowered us to collectively challenge the experts and fight for acceptance. We believe that gender identity and gender expression are such profound concepts that only a person who truly lives a gender non-conforming life can possibly explain our intensely-held feelings.

If you picked up this book to help understand someone you care about who is transgender, you are an important ally in our quest for acceptance. Without allies like you who have read the information in this book, people tend to make up damaging stories about transgender people that are not based in fact.

So how could my background in accounting and finance possibly make me qualified to write about the subject? First, accounting is itself a complex subject, and my work has required me to become proficient at explaining it in ways that others can understand. Transgender is an equally complex subject.

More importantly, the analytical mind that makes me competent as an accountant also forced me to intensely question my first notion in 2002 that I needed to transition genders. True, I had felt the gender incongruity very early in my life, yet I had intensely denied those feelings for much of my life, as explained in my chapter "Mutual Transformation." Once I suspected that I was transgender, I started reading every book I could on the subject—clinical works, history, fiction, and memoirs—and I continue to read new works as they come out. Through this book, you benefit from my reading without having to read all of those books yourself. I do point out my ten favorite books at the end of the book for those who want to do further reading.

In all of my writing I use "transgender" in the broadest, most inclusionary way, as explained in Chapter 1. There are many types of people included under the transgender umbrella. One surprise for most readers will be that many under that umbrella do not have surgery. For that reason, I rarely talk about my own situation in my explanations to avoid any unintended false implication that surgery is the goal of all.

Some transgender people do not see their gender as clearly male or female, while others see it as bits of both male and female. I am part of yet another group that finds our gender to be clearly the opposite of what we were assigned at birth. I am fortunate in that I could afford the hormones and surgery, none of it covered by insurance, to bring my appearance in line with my deeply held belief of being female. While I have chosen to be visible as a transgender woman, most who believe as I do and can afford the medical costs choose to blend in as their desired gender and therefore disappear from the transgender population.

The problem with this is that the ones who cannot blend in, either because they do not view gender as simply binary (male/female) or who do see gender as binary but cannot afford the medical costs, are likely to face job discrimination as a result. The fight for transgender acceptance is greatly hindered because it has to depend upon these underemployed and unemployed members of the community for funding.

If only we could convince those who have blended in to share some of their success to help those less fortunate. Contributing dollars to efforts for transgender acceptance would help, of course, but visibility as successful transgender people would be even better. Of course, this has to be done very carefully in areas that have yet to outlaw discrimination against transgender people (unfortunately still over 60% of the country), but there may be "safe" opportunities there, too.

I'm not suggesting going on *Oprah* or marching in a picket line, nor am I suggesting they reveal their transgender status to every new person they meet. I am suggesting, however, that they take advantage of small opportunities that come up—say when a good friend is talking about a transgender character on the TV drama *CSI*—to calmly and patiently educate.

During my time on the Board of Directors of GLAD, I saw that one of the keys to winning the right to same sex-marriage in five New England states was for people to meet the gay couple next door. People now need to meet the transgender person who has been living next door all this time and who they never knew was transgender.

But please note: you should never reveal someone's transgender status against their will as the risks are too great until transgender people are protected at the federal level from employment discrimination and hate crimes. But you can be of great help by offering steadfast support to the transgender person in your life, so that they can feel safe if they choose to be visible as a transgender. Even a little bit of visibility will help.

I also encourage you to you meet other transgender people. There is no substitute for meeting others and hearing their personal views on the topics in my book. I suspect you will find that, in spite of our individual differences, we are all largely like any other person next door, interested in many of the same basic things you are, and just wanting to go about our everyday lives as ourselves just like you do.

THE PRIMER

1. The Basics: What It Means to be Transgender or Gender Non-Conforming

In the next eight hundred or so words, I'll summarize the key things you need to know. I'll include references in the text where another chapter provides more information on a particular topic. But if you read only one chapter in this book, this is the one to read.

Let's start with terminology. Individuals with an alternate gender identity (how you feel) and/or gender expression (how you look and act) often get referred to as "transgender" for expediency.

Unfortunately, because of the stigma associated with any adjective beginning with "trans," many people affected by issues related to their gender identity or expression nonetheless deny being transgender. These people include the man or boy whose feminine behavior provokes catcalls or bullying, the masculine woman or girl who gets harassed when she uses the ladies' room, the gay individual who occasionally dresses in drag (in clothes of the opposite gender), and the intersex (Chapter 3) person born with any one of a number of conditions that make their anatomical sex inconsistent or ambiguous.

Those who are more classically included under the transgender umbrella (Chapter 2) include transsexuals who transition genders as I did, heterosexual cross-dressers who have an opposite gender presentation only part of the time, and genderqueer people who have a unique gender presentation all of the time.

Sexual orientation (who you love) has no relation to any of this. As an example, I am still attracted to women in my new life while my two best friends, also trans women, are now attracted to men. I am therefore gay but my friends are straight.

What is the prevalence (Chapter 4) of transgenderism and gender non-conformity? For many years, all we had to go on were the low numbers from the American Psychiatric Association dating from the decades-old beginnings of transgender understanding. But trans woman Prof. Lynn Conway, a brilliant computer scientist who developed technology used in most computers today, applied her analytical smarts a few years ago to come up with a better estimate: 1.5 percent of the population, or fifteen people per thousand in the population. Comparing with the Williams Institute's latest statistic for gay/lesbian prevalence, that's one person for every three gay/lesbian people.

If that seems too high, it could be because transgender people have been highly closeted in the past. Those who transitioned genders often chose to live "stealth" (Chapter 5) in their new gender—never admitting to being transgender—because of safety concerns, societal stigma, and prejudice. And as GenderPAC executive director, Riki Wilchins, observed in a 2008 Advocate.com commentary, even the gay rights movement previously forced gender-nonconforming gays into hiding to make the argument "that we are 'just like everyone else' except that we sleep with same-sex partners."

Part of the stigma about being trans comes from the fact that gender identity disorder is still in the American Psychiatric Association's catalog of mental disorders. Why hasn't it been removed given that homosexuality was removed in 1973? Because for those of us who need hormones and surgery to feel authentic in our new genders, paternalistic medical guidelines (Chapter 6) still require a GID diagnosis. Some believe that the diagnosis enables doctors to provide treatment when they might fear accusations of malpractice without it.

Another source of the stigma is what I call MIDS: Man in a Dress Syndrome (Chapter 16). Women were essentially required thirty years ago to cross-dress—in masculine-looking skirt suits—to gain entrance into corporate America. But even today, when a man puts on the clothes of a woman, he is immediately presumed less capable. Sadly, this is not the only way in which overt sexism (Chapter 19) skews perceptions of transgender people.

Only 37 percent of Americans live in areas explicitly banning discrimination (Chapter 10) based on gender identity and expression according to the latest statistic from the National Center for Transgender Equality. In areas lacking protection, a simple no-match letter (Chapter 11) from the Social Security Administration stating that the gender in its database does not match the one you listed in your employment application can provoke your employer to fire you.

That's sad, because transgender people can be very capable employees. There are many success stories (Chapter 14). Fortunately, acceptance in corporate America (Chapter

13) is growing rapidly. The Corporate Equality Index of the Human Rights Campaign has registered stunning increases in the number of major U.S. businesses banning discrimination based on gender identity and expression. If there is such a groundswell of support, why then did lawmakers exclude gender identity and expression from the 2007 House bill (called ENDA) to outlaw employment discrimination?

The answer is that conservative religious activists have been busy learning everything about transgenderism and gender non-conformity so they can twist the facts and scare the lawmakers. Legislators need to know that trans issues are not a new ploy in the "homosexual agenda." Quite the contrary: Transgender people were visible in everyday life in the Bible (Chapter 17), along with evidence that Jesus wanted us included too.

2. Sub-Groups Under the Transgender Umbrella

Back in the 1980s, Billy Crystal's Fernando character on *Saturday Night Live* claimed, "It's not how you feel, it's how you look!" He was on the right track, except that how one feels can be equally important, as you will see.

What image comes to mind when someone says transgender? RuPaul, the model and singer-songwriter? Eddie Izzard, the Emmy winning British stand-up comedian and actor? Bree, Felicity Huffman's character in the movie *Transamerica*? Leslie Feinberg or Kate Bornstein?

These are all examples of people whose gender expression (how one looks) and gender identity (how one feels) can be problematic in a pink or blue society. Actually, problematic is an understatement. Every month, more than one person is murdered just for being gender-nonconforming—and those are only the cases we know about. This grim figure represents a strikingly large percentage of a relatively small and little-understood population.

In the late 1980s, the word transgender was coined as an umbrella term to refer to all gender non-conforming people. That's one expansive umbrella! It covers drag queens and drag kings, cross-dressers, transsexuals, and genderqueer people. Men and women with nontraditional gender expressions are usually protected by trans-inclusive nondiscrimination and employment laws even if they do not use the transgender label.

Recognizing the common struggle for civil rights—and the common opponents—the gay and lesbian movement started adding the T to make it LGBT in the mid 1990s. But my experience has been that even the average gay man or lesbian today knows very little about the transgender community and truly wants to know more, just like most others.

So please allow me shed a little light on trans terminology.

RuPaul is probably the best known example of a drag queen. Drag kings—women who perform in a male persona—are growing in popularity too; Heywood Wakefield is one example. (Drag originally meant "DRessed As a Girl," but for those dressing as a boy, drab didn't exactly draw an audience!) People who "do drag" do it for fun, entertainment, and sometimes to earn a livelihood. Drag queens and kings are generally gay or bisexual, and few ever feel the need to medically transition genders as actress Alexis Arquette did. So, for the drag community, the issue is their right to their gender expression.

Wikipedia says Izzard "regularly cross-dresses both on and off stage and makes it clear that cross-dressing is neither a part of his performance nor a sexual thing—he simply enjoys wearing make-up and clothing that is traditionally perceived in the West as female-only." Women started wearing men's clothes awhile ago as a fashion statement, and today that is commonplace. But when a guy puts on a dress, it's still a huge deal! So men who have a yet-to-be-explained need to cross-dress often have to limit their dressing to the privacy of their homes or to one of the various transgender conferences held around the country each year. Cross-dressers are usually straight in the gender they were assigned at birth, and few feel the need to medically transition. Regardless of the reasons why they cross-dress, the issue is their right to their gender expression.

Bree (Felicity Huffman's character) is an example of a "transsexual," as am I. We represent the small part of the transgender population who feels so strongly about being the gender opposite of our original sex organs that—if we can afford it—we take medical steps (hormone therapy and/or surgery) to bring our physical bodies (how we look) into alignment with our gender identity (how we feel).

Many others who have a strong contra-gender identity also "transition" to live in their preferred gender, using clothing, makeup, and mannerisms but without transitioning medically. Many are unable to afford hormones or surgery because transgender health care is still not covered by most insurance plans. Still others fear medical procedures or shun them on principle. Increasingly, non-medical transitioners are also referred to as transsexual.

Transsexual people can be lesbian, gay, bisexual, or straight; I identify as lesbian. Our issue is our right to both our gender expression and gender identity.

Leslie Feinberg and Kate Bornstein are real-life examples of the rest of the transgender population. For them, the gender binary (male/female) does not work for their daily lives, either in part or in the whole. It happens that both are writers, and Feinberg's *Stone Butch Blues* and Bornstein's *Gender Outlaw* are often included in college gender studies curricula these days because they encourage the reader to reconsider the entrenched gender binary.

Perhaps as a result of being exposed to these writings in college, there is an increase in younger people coming out as "genderqueer," which they pretty much define however they want. It can mean identifying as some of one gender and part of another or even identifying as none of the above. Their issue is their right to both their gender expression and gender identity.

So what about you? You likely don't consider yourself transgender. But is how you feel and how you look important to you? A woman does not think of herself as a man (identity) when she wears a tie (expression), nor does a feminine man think of himself as a woman because of his actions.

Unlike what Billy Crystal's character purported, how one feels and how one acts and looks are critical to one's self-definition. And regardless of whether you consider yourself transgender, we likely have common concerns that give us a good reason to work for transgender acceptance.

3. Intersex

The woman giving the presentation at the front of the room is as curvy as can be. So imagine my surprise when she reveals that she has XY chromosomes and has not had surgery to create those curves! Yet she did have surgery at birth to remove her undescended testes long before she was capable of authorizing the surgery. What in the world is going on here?

Welcome to the world of intersex people. The Intersex Society of North America describes an intersex condition as being "born with an anatomy that someone decided is not standard male or female." Many intersex people have "normalizing" surgeries imposed on them when they are too young to grant permission and then spend the rest of their lives struggling to heal from those surgeries.

In that struggle, they often encounter issues based upon their gender identity and gender expression, and those struggles sometimes result in intersex people being included under the transgender umbrella. Whether or not that is appropriate, their situation is certainly worth a few words. (And if you ever see "LGBTI," this is the I.)

There are many different types of intersex conditions. These conditions can result in women without ovaries, clitorises, and/or inner labia, and men without testes. They include people whose genitals are ambiguous, and people with chromosomes that are neither XX nor XY. They also include any baby with testicles whose penis is too short, and any baby without testicles whose clitoris is too large.

Biologist Anne Fausto-Sterling has estimated that one or two of every thousand births have surgery to "normalize" genital appearance long before the children understand what is going on. Parents authorize the surgeries, desperate to avoid the "shame" of a child who does not conform to the gender binary, and the medical profession is only too happy to comply. Doctors then instruct parents to socialize the child as the gender that the child was made into, which, as you might guess, is disproportionately female. Parents are told to never tell the child about the surgery. Call it "Spin Control, Home Edition."

This flawed treatment protocol is based largely on work done at Johns Hopkins University in the 1950s and 1960s, which purported to show nurture was more important than nature in raising a child. We have since learned that people have a very strong perception of the gender they are—their gender identity—regardless of their upbringing. And a high-profile case that initially served as support for the Hopkins work—of a boy raised as a girl after a botched circumcision—later took a dramatic turn to make it convincing evidence to the contrary.

The story of David Reimer is documented in John Colapinto's 2000 biography *As Nature Made Him*. All the while that David was being referred to as a success story by Johns Hopkins psychologist John Money, David was clearly uncomfortable living as a girl and was refusing the recommended subsequent surgery to create a vagina. When David learned the truth about his botched circumcision at age 14, he quickly transitioned to live as a boy.

A 2004 study, conducted by another scientist at Johns Hopkins and published in *The New England Journal of Medicine*, offered more proof challenging the supposed success of nurturing intersex children into a specific gender identity. The study followed sixteen cases of children who were genetically and hormonally male but were born with a very small or absent penis. Of the sixteen, fourteen were given female hormones and raised as girls. Years later, researchers found all sixteen to be behaving as boys no matter how they were raised, with eight of them now declaring themselves male.

What causes intersexuality? It's often just the normal course of nature—there's much more gender and sex diversity in the human species than we were taught in school. But there is also evidence showing that exposure to certain chemicals while *in utero* can alter physical and genetic sex. Deborah Rudacille explores this possibility at length in her excellent book *The Riddle of Gender* (one of the Ten Books I Recommend in Chapter 28). She cites, for example, the surprising tendency of the sons of moms who took the synthetic estrogen supplement DES during pregnancy to have intersex conditions.

Intersex people who ultimately learn (and most do) that they underwent "normalizing" surgeries are left to feel as if they are anything but normal as a result. They feel rejected as the people they were at birth. They are also hindered in developing intimate relationships because the surgeries usually damage sexual sensation. And should the gender imposed on them in their early years turn out to be the wrong one, they often feel no choice but to undergo a gender transition to undo a choice that their parents and the medical community made for them.

Intersex people provide us with a compelling example of how a strict, unwavering adherence to the gender binary can cause far more damage than good.

4. Prevalence: There Are More of Us Than You Think

Next time you find yourself in a crowd of five thousand people consider this: In the crowd there will be on average one person living with muscular dystrophy. There will also be on average two people who have already undergone male-to-female sex-reassignment surgery. And there may as many as seventy-five in that crowd who are transgender or gender non-conforming. Are you surprised?

For years, the only statistics available on transgender prevalence were those first developed in the 1960s and 1970s. These statistics, as still cited in the American Psychiatric Association's most recent *Diagnostic and Statistics Manual*, DSM-IV, "suggest that roughly one per 30,000 adult males and one per 100,000 adult females seek [sex-reassignment surgery]."

Thank goodness Prof. Lynn Conway could not believe these low numbers. Lynn is a noted computer scientist and distinguished professor emerita of engineering who transitioned from male to female (MTF) in the 1960s and then lived "stealth," or closeted about her transgender status, before coming out in 2000 (more about stealth and

Lynn in upcoming chapters). Shortly after her coming-out, Lynn turned her highly analytical brain toward understanding the statistics.

Her skepticism was based on simple reasoning. If the psychiatrists were right, there would be only three or four thousand MTFs in the United States who had ever sought surgery. Under the optimistic assumption that only 20 percent or so would have been able to afford or attain surgery, there would be fewer than eight hundred postoperative women in the country today. Impossible, she cried, given that the top sex-reassignment surgery surgeons in the United States alone perform that many MTF SRS operations every single year.

Lynn then extended her logic to come up with much more realistic and believable numbers for transsexuals and then the entire transgender and gender non-conforming population (including the numbers mentioned at the start of this chapter), revealing large errors in the psychiatrists' old claims. All of Lynn's reasoning and estimates are detailed on her tremendously valuable Web site, www.lynnconway. com.

In 2007, Conway and fellow PhD Femke Olyslager presented to WPATH (the World Professional Association for Transgender Health) an updated analysis showing that an even greater prevalence is likely. Yet the APA (American Psychiatric Association) has continued to show its bias by ignoring this analysis and misinterpreting other research in its 2008 report of the APA Task Force on Gender Identity and Gender Variance.

Why don't we have better official numbers? Lynn postulates that (a) psychiatrists don't question the numbers because they don't see the significant number of transsexuals who manage to transition without their "help," and (b) because more accurate numbers showing a much larger prevalence would be bad for the psychiatry business and its bias toward marginalizing transsexualism as an extremely rare mental illness.

So what about statistics for female-to-male (FTM) trans people? The old official stats imply that there are less than a third as many FTMs as MTFs. I used to believe that. After all, when I first started attending transgender conferences, the attendees were overwhelmingly individuals presenting as female. And then one day, wanting to know more about the seemingly elusive FTMs, I read Jamison Green's fabulous book, *Becoming a Visible Man* (one of the Ten Books I Recommend in Chapter 28).

James is a charismatic (and handsome, even to this lesbian) writer and activist who transitioned FTM in the late 1980s. In his book, James states the obvious: FTMs were simply not interested in the feminine grooming tips and female hormones being discussed in conferences and support groups that largely catered to MTF trans people. But gender counseling providers assumed the groups had broader appeal and that the men actually stayed away to be self-sufficient like "other" men. This became self-perpetuating when the professionals actively told patients that men "like to go it alone."

James showed how this thinking deprived FTMs of role models and, more importantly, of an awareness of just how many others were out there. Fortunately the treatment of FTMs is much less monolithic these days, and FTMs have learned that "communication among men does not threaten their independence." There are now FTM-centric conferences like True Spirit and Gender Odyssey, and FTMs are now quite visible in the lesbian, gay, bisexual and transgender (LGBT) community and on college campuses across the country. Current thinking is that the prevalence of FTMs is much closer to the prevalence of MTFs.

But my fellow board members at Point Foundation, none of whom is transgender (why? See Chapter 21), are convinced that there are considerably more FTMs. We award scholarships to undergraduate and graduate students whom we feel will be the LGBT leaders of tomorrow. Our evaluation process is rigorous. That process has resulted in fifteen of the nearly 150 scholarships to date (as of 2009) going to transgender and gender non-conforming students, eleven of whom are FTM. I am continually stunned to see that well over 80 percent of the applications each year are from FTMs. Where are all the MTFs?

I asked Lynn Conway, who as a professor emerita spends a fair amount of time on college campuses, for her take on this. Lynn points out that while accepting of girls who present as tomboys, our society still has incredibly deep hang-ups about boys presenting in a feminine way. This stigmatization results in an alarming number of young MTF kids being thrown away or disowned by their parents, even before they reach college age.

Of the MTFs who do manage to enter college, the vast majority remain totally closeted so as to avoid ostracism. Lynn also notes that some campus LGBT offices remain dominated by second-wave feminist thinking, which tends to look askance at anyone who appears to them to preserve feminine stereotypes (read more on this in Chapter 20). Although such offices may honor the FTM in transition, they often aren't places where young MTFs feel welcome, leading to a big asymmetry in visible numbers on campuses.

It is situations like this that limit awareness of the size of the transgender population. There actually are a lot of us, and only when the transgender stigma finally crumbles will everyone finally see all of us.

5. "Stealth": Out of One Closet and Into Another

During Bree and Toby's road trip in the 2005 movie *Transamerica*, Bree arranges for both of them to stay at a friend's home in Dallas on the evening they pass through. Upon arrival, Bree is positively shocked to find her friend's living room filled with her transgender friends gathered for a social evening. Bree looks to her hostess in panic and whispers, "My friend told me you were stealth!"

Stealth essentially means living fully and completely in your true gender but never, ever admitting to be transgender. Think of it as the transgender version of "covering," the subject and title of Kenji Yoshino's thought-provoking 2006 book. In our case, it usually requires leaving your past behind. Your previous distinguished service as an F-4 Phantom pilot in Vietnam might be a tad difficult to explain as a woman, as is undoubtedly the case for American Airlines pilot Sara Weston. Similarly, your intimate familiarity with motherhood might seem puzzling coming from a man. Living stealth can also require leaving behind family, friends, colleagues, and anyone else who might out you to others.

So, why come out of one closet only to step into another?

The dangers facing out trans people were once so severe that stealth used to be part of the standard treatment protocol prescribed by professionals for those needing to transition genders. In fact, I have a friend who was forced in 1994 to divorce from her spouse to accomplish her transition, in spite of having a healthy relationship and two children. Fortunately, stealth is optional these days. Yet many still actively choose stealth to avoid the societal stigma, prejudice, and the safety concerns that come with being an out transgender person.

Stealth is essentially a second closet, with all of the issues associated with being in a closet. Stealth is much harder to maintain when you are with other transgender people, because very slight gender incongruities in one person can be overlooked but when two or more gender non-conforming people are in the same space such details easily arouse suspicion. Bree had assumed that her friend had broken all ties with her trans friends in order to remain stealth, and when that was clearly not the case, she panicked, thinking Toby would quickly figure her out. He did.

Most people who are stealth are just so happy to be finally living in their true gender that all of the hassle is tolerated. But for a few, the difficulty and loneliness of essentially starting over, without a personal history or connections with the trans community, leaves them depressed and despondent. Outsiders may interpret this heartache as meaning that transitioning genders had been a mistake for the person when being stealth was actually the mistake, albeit forced by the former treatment standards, stigma avoidance, and/or very real safety concerns. Read more about regret in Chapter 15.

It's also much harder to succeed at being stealth if you lack privilege, which comes in many forms. It includes having the economic means to afford the hormones and/ or surgeries that make your body and face appear more traditionally feminine or masculine. Or having bodily size and features that are not out of normal range for the new gender. In this aspect I am privileged. For example, at 5 foot 9, I am right at the level of tall non-transgender women. But many of my trans women friends are considerably taller!

Privilege also includes being heterosexual in the new gender, as you can imagine. Here I am not privileged, although I did have mitigating circumstances. I transitioned from straight male to transgender lesbian female. However, my late wife Barbara willingly and lovingly stayed with me through my 2002 transition until her death in 2006, essentially delaying my assimilation of my lesbian status.

And, of course, privilege includes being a white person in a racist society. People of color face discrimination whether transgender or not, and that makes going stealth—finding a new job, securing housing, and accessing services—all the more difficult. Trans people unable to get medical care might buy hormones on the street, increasing the likelihood of sharing needles and greatly increasing the risk of contracting hepatitis C or HIV.

People of color also unfairly face greater police scrutiny whether transgender or not, which increases the likelihood of being incarcerated. Many prisons provide neither hormones nor any other aspects of transgender health care, and that can trigger severe depression in trans prisoners. When transgender health care *is* provided in prison, the media like to report it as a frivolous waste of taxpayer dollars.

Furthermore, because the laws remain hung up on whether one has had surgery, a transgender prisoner is far more likely to be put into a cell based upon anatomical sex without regard to gender identity or presentation. For those who have not had, don't desire, or can't afford surgery, this housing policy is extremely dangerous. There have been many stories of trans prisoners who have been beaten and raped by other inmates or, incredibly, by prison guards themselves.

Because of all of these institutionalized oppressions, and because of the media's fondness for stories of the downtrodden, your image of the transgender population may be rather skewed. Varying degrees of stealth have allowed a lot of trans people to be successful in spite of these challenges, while being fairly invisible to you. A few of us have even been successful while being out as transgender. I encourage you to read about some of those success stories in Chapter 14. Your image of transgender people will never be the same.

6. If it's Not a Mental Illness, Why is it Still in the *DSM?*

As a transsexual woman, I have a mental disorder, or so says the current *Diagnostic and Statistics Manual of Mental Disorders, Fourth Edition* (*DSM IV*) of the American Psychiatric Association. My diagnosis code is 302.85—Gender Identity Disorder of Adolescence of Adulthood (GID).

Gay men and lesbians used to have a mental disorder too. That was true until homosexuality was removed from the *DSM* in 1973. Why am I still in the big book of mental disorders so many years later?

It's a very complicated matter, due in part to the existence of "The Standards of Care for Gender Identity Disorders" (SOC) of the World Professional Association for Transgender Health. WPATH—a group of medical doctors, psychologists, and other professionals—developed the SOC as a set of guidelines for diagnosing and treating people like me. The complication arises because the SOC require that a person have a diagnosis of Gender Identity Disorder as defined in the *DSM IV* in order to access treatment. Most ethical professionals in this and other countries use the SOC as a guide, so the *DSM IV* diagnosis is a necessary step on the road to transition.

Specifically, the SOC recommend a minimum of three months of psychotherapy before the therapist will write a letter permitting access to hormones. During that time the therapist confirms that the patient has GID and not something else. Once passing that hurdle, the SOC recommend that the patient live in the perceived gender for at least a year before the therapist writes a letter granting access to sex reassignment surgery. That letter must be countersigned by a psychiatrist or PhD psychologist.

Think of the SOC as a box that pops up on the computer screen of life, saying, "Are you really, really sure you want to change your gender?" This irks a lot of transsexual people, many of whom have (or had) felt at odds with our sex from a young age. We point out that what little research has been done suggests the incongruity originated while we were being carried in our mothers' wombs. Why is some costly expert required to confirm an uncomfortable reality that is not of our doing and that we've been living for all of these years? In the current social context, where gender difference is still seen as negative, a diagnosis of mental illness further stigmatizes transsexual people as sick and in need of a "cure" rather than equal civil rights.

Gender identity disorder is in the *DSM IV* in a way that includes those "who may or may not be transsexual and who may or may not be distressed or impaired," according to Dr. Kelley Winters of GID Reform Advocates. And the *DSM IV* also includes another diagnosis—302.3, called Transvestic Fetishism, which labels cross-dressing by heterosexual males as sexual fetish and paraphilia.

Winters thinks there's something fishy about these *DSM IV* diagnoses, though. In her painstakingly-researched 2009 book, *Gender Madness in American Psychiatry: Essays From the Struggle for Dignity* (one of the Ten Books I Recommend in Chapter 28), Winters discovered that 1) The diagnoses that label trans people as mentally ill are based largely upon the opinion of a handful of non-transgender psychiatrists imposing their view of what is socially acceptable behavior. 2) These psychiatrists base their opinion almost entirely on studies of their own patients without considering the large number of transgender people leading well-adjusted lives who don't feel the need to see a psychiatrist. 3) These psychiatrists are suspiciously relentless in challenging the credibility of anyone who seeks to challenge their opinion. 4) Their opinion ignores significant studies by other professionals showing that most individuals who transition genders have positive outcomes. 5) The diagnoses are written in a way that remove the mental illness label for a patient who undergoes reparative therapy (which claims to make an individual not transgender) but not for a patient who transitions genders, even if the outcome is positive. And 6) Some of these same psychiatrists happen to specialize in reparative therapy and therefore have a vested interest in labeling trans people as mentally ill.

In her book, Winters documents how the *DSM IV* diagnoses of the American Psychiatric Association came to be and why reform is needed. She carefully shows that the diagnoses are based more upon variance from societal norms than distress or impairment caused by gender dysphoria (discontent with the sex assigned at one's birth). Winters demonstrates how this official view of the APA is used to justify job terminations and other types of discrimination.

Herein lies the big catch-22. The SOC essentially represent a medicalized approach to treatment, involving hormone therapy or surgery. And yet, because the *DSM IV* labels a person as mentally ill, most health insurance plans will not pay for any treatment for a GID diagnosis code. This means that a patient who is diagnosed with GID may end up without access to treatment solely because they cannot afford to pay the costs out of pocket.

The exclusion in health insurance plans of all treatments related to sex reassignment is terribly unfair. Insurers will cover a hysterectomy for a female who has uterine cancer, but they won't cover the same surgery for a female-bodied person who is transitioning to fit a deeply held male gender identity—even when it is recommended by a doctor for the psychological well-being of the transgender patient.

Costs are usually cited as the reason, but this is unjustifiable. When a San Francisco ordinance expanded health care coverage to transgender employees in 2001, premiums for all city employees were raised to cover the feared spike in costs. Mark Leno, an ordinance sponsor who went on to become a California assemblyman, said three years after the new coverage was instituted, "The revenues to pay for care exceeded costs by a factor of twenty-five, demonstrating that concerns about spiraling costs were misplaced." Two corporations providing transgender health coverage during the same period, Avaya and Lucent, similarly experienced much lower than expected costs.

There's another, more fundamental problem with the GID diagnosis: it assumes the gender binary as a foundation. What if you define or express your gender in a way that doesn't quite fit the binary? Or what if you don't desire hormone therapy or surgery to feel comfortable expressing your gender identity? You likely will not be diagnosed as having GID, meaning you too will be denied treatment.

So why not remove GID from the *DSM IV*? Aside from its existence as the linchpin of the SOC, some believe that its presence gives doctors a basis for providing hormones and surgery for us when they might fear being accused of malpractice otherwise. For those of us who truly need(ed) and want(ed) hormones and surgery, the prospect of having no doctors available to carry out the treatments is downright scary. So we remain in the *DSM*, many years after homosexuality was removed.

But really, isn't it the very presence of GID in the *DSM IV* that leads to the fear of malpractice in the first place? If so, the question is how to manage removing GID from the *DSM IV* in a way that allows trans people access to some level of treatment as the standards are reformed. This could take a while given that some of the psychiatrists who helped develop the *DSM IV* diagnoses, and who have a vested interest in maintaining them, have lead roles in the development of the *DSM V*, which will be released in 2012.

7. Common Procedures Male-to-Female

(Note: There are serious risks to any hormone therapies. They should not be undertaken in the absence of a knowledgeable doctor's ongoing supervision.)

Forgive me while I dip into my prior (male) life for a proper analogy to describe what it was like to have the wrong primary sex hormone coursing through my body. The only way to explain it is that I felt like a car running on the wrong type of gas. I did not fully understand how wrong it was until I replaced testosterone with estrogen when I transitioned genders in 2002. I now have an amazing sense of well-being and harmony that I never knew before. Now my body just hums.

Estrogen has also accomplished physical changes that contribute to my harmony. Because I now carry a higher body fat content, as other women do, my skin feels softer, and I have a few curves I didn't have before. Of course, all the curves in the world couldn't hide my broader shoulders and longer waist, but they help. My rear end is larger now too but still a little smaller than my ideal. In fact, I have on occasion joked with my non-trans women friends that I would gladly trade my shoulders for their butts.

One thing estrogen cannot do is make a male voice rise into female range. There are surgeries that claim to be able to do this, but their success rates are terrible, and because the procedures can actually cause damage, they are not recommended. The safer alternative is voice therapy, the results of which can be quite good. Remember the voice coach at the very opening of the movie *Transamerica*? Many MTFs know about Andrea James, and some (including me) own her voice course. There are also speech therapists in larger cities that specialize in voice feminization.

Estrogen may make your body hair softer, but it does not get rid of hair in the places women usually don't have hair. For this reason, many people seek electrolysis. In my case, I had so much hair to remove that I chose to make several trips to a legendary establishment, well-known in the MTF community, where they use external injections of anesthetics to permit extended electrolysis sessions. It took five days with two technicians working on me from 9:00 am to 5:00 pm to remove my facial hair, and three hundred hours of electrolysis overall. Others require less and can get by seeing the local electrologist, but it still adds up to a significant expense.

Estrogen also does not grow hair in the places where women normally have hair. If you transition genders later in life, chances are you are suffering from male pattern baldness. Some have luck re-growing hair with hair re-growth medications, but more severe baldness usually requires hair transplantation or a hairpiece in order to meet expectations for feminine hair.

And, of course, estrogen does not give you female sex organs. This is where some turn to sex-reassignment surgery. I say some because many people under the transgender umbrella can't afford SRS, and some never feel the need for it. Really! Some achieve harmony with their gender identity after following a few or all of the steps above without SRS, while others are satisfied just by living as the opposite gender, or somewhere in between, all of the time or maybe even some of the time.

Our culture and our laws, however, are very focused on SRS as the defining moment that one switches genders. For example, while the movie *Transamerica* was generally well done, the advertising and publicity annoyed many of us by referring to the main character Bree as "he" in the days prior to her SRS, even though she was living as a woman. Meanwhile, the gender marker on most legal documents cannot be changed without proof of SRS. This is highly problematic for transgender people who need to have legal identification that matches their gender identity and outward appearance. Besides, why are we forced to disclose what is or is not in our pants in the first place?

But since SRS is of great interest to many, I'll outline the common procedure for MTFs, called vaginoplasty. As described in Wikipedia, "the erectile tissue of the penis is removed, and the skin, with its blood and nerve supplies still attached, is inverted into a cavity created in the pelvis. Part of the tip, still connected to its blood and nerve supplies, is usually used to construct a clitoris, and the urethra is shortened to end at a place that is appropriate for a female anatomy."

After sex reassignment surgery, one can have vaginal intercourse but, of course, cannot give birth. I've been told that 85 percent of those who have had SRS can achieve orgasm. It often takes a while after surgery, however, to learn what stimulation (and where) works with your new anatomy. MTF SRS can cost as much as $20,000 and require three to four weeks of time off, and unless you are very active sexually it requires dilating the vagina at least once a week for the rest of your life to keep it from closing up. It is not a surgery to be undertaken lightly.

At the same time as SRS, or separately, some may opt for additional procedures to enhance outward appearance. Some choose breast augmentation if estrogen therapy has not resulted in adequate breast tissue growth. Others may undergo a "tracheal shave," a surgical procedure which generally successfully minimizes the prominence of the Adam's apple.

Ironically, hormone therapy and SRS are usually not allowed without the authorization of a mental health professional, yet few insurance plans cover any aspect of transgender care. Cost is usually cited as the concern, fueled by the false belief that all transgender people want SRS. The result is that beneficial estrogen therapy, covered without question for the well-being of a menopausal woman, is generally not covered for the well-being of a transgender woman. How sad.

8. Common Procedures Female-to-Male

(Note: There are serious risks to any hormone therapies. They should not be undertaken in the absence of a knowledgeable doctor's ongoing supervision.)

If you have male gender identity but were born female-bodied, you may determine that testosterone therapy can help you realize your true physical self. Once on testosterone, my female-to-male friends report the same sense of well-being and harmony that my male-to-female friends experience on estrogen therapy. But the effects of the two hormones could not be more different.

In addition to my own observations, I have relied on the terrific book *Becoming a Visible Man* (one of the Ten Books I Recommend in Chapter 28), written by one of the most visible FTM activists, Jamison Green, for this chapter.

Within a few months of starting your FTM testosterone therapy, your voice will drop irreversibly. In time you will also find hair growing in places where men normally have hair, both on your body and your face. You may even find your hairline starting to recede. All of these are welcome developments—except maybe for the balding—that provide "gender clues" helpful to the general public in perceiving you as a male. You're off to a good start.

There are some other effects of FTM testosterone therapy that are less visible to the public but just as welcome. Most noticeably, your menstruation will stop. Menstruation, and especially all of those tampons and pads, served as an annoying monthly reminder of the incongruity between your body and your head. Testosterone will also cause your body's pores to enlarge, and that will make your skin feel appropriately rougher. Your body fat will redistribute to the stomach and away from the hips so that the symbolic beer gut can now be more easily achieved (although that's not for everyone, of course).

Some effects of testosterone are not so welcome. One visible effect can be acne, even in older trans men. If a doctor is overseeing your hormone therapy, and hopefully that is the case, she or he can help control your acne. More significantly, your LDL cholesterol level will likely increase, possibly enough to require cholesterol-reducing dietary habits, medication, or medical supervision.

An effect that seems to have surprised many of my FTM friends is the increase in sex drive and enjoyment. It's not that they hadn't expected or even desired the change; it's just that it was way more intense than they imagined. Personally, as one who has gone the other direction, I'm delighted that sex is no longer my number one priority each day. Of course, I am wired female, so it is now very clear how testosterone was tampering with my natural inclinations. It's powerful stuff, believe me.

But testosterone does nothing about your breasts, which probably clash with your desired masculine appearance. Many FTMs bind their breasts to hide them, but this doesn't help when your friends invite you to the beach. Binding is also terribly uncomfortable and can actually cause injury over time. Therefore, some choose "top surgery," a special kind of mastectomy where your breast tissue is removed and your chest and nipples are contoured to create a male appearance. Depending on the procedure performed and your family history, you may still need to have periodic screenings for breast cancer. Unfortunately, many mammography labs, as well as the patients in their waiting rooms, have a way to go before they understand why you would want to be a patient.

For some FTMs it is important to have the nonvisible female reproductive organs removed, both to feel most comfortable in their bodies and because there has been little research done on the impact of testosterone therapy on those organs. This procedure can be a good idea if you have a family history of disease in that area, and if, as a man, you want to avoid the otherwise recommended visits to a gynecologist.

Of course, testosterone does nothing to give you male sex organs. This is where choices get difficult for FTMs. There are two surgical options, each with issues, so "bottom surgery" is rarely pursued. Neither procedure is covered by insurance.

The more commonly chosen option is called metoidioplasty. This procedure involves releasing your clitoris, which has become enlarged by testosterone. A scrotum can be formed by joining your labia majora and using silicone testicular implants. The result is a significantly smaller-than-average penis, although it is sexually sensitive and does get erect. The cost can run up to $20,000.

The other option is phalloplasty. In this procedure a flap of skin is taken, usually from your forearm or thigh, and fashioned into a penis that is attached above your clitoris. If implants are not used to create erection, a stent may be required to erect your shaft. The resulting penis is more average in size but is less natural looking and may not be sexually sensitive. The procedure is also riskier and more expensive—up to $40,000, not including the costs of revisions that are usually required.

In either procedure, some doctors will perform a urethral extension through your penis, although the techniques are not yet perfected. The urethral extension will typically allow you to stand at the men's room urinal.

As in the case of MTFs, the laws are unfairly focused on surgery as the defining moment that one switches gender. Many locales have accepted top surgery as sex-reassignment surgery, but some are now requiring more. This is a highly problematic state of affairs when the additional surgeries available for FTMs are expensive, not covered by insurance, can produce results that are unacceptable, and can be risky. How sad, when testosterone alone can produce the gender clues that society reads as male.

9. Transgender Children

I didn't realize my need to transition to female until I was age forty-seven. When I did transition, it was long after puberty had given me a male face, male-pattern baldness, and a male voice in the bass range. I have had to spend a fair amount of time, effort, and money in my new life as a woman to overcome these male gender clues. How great would it have been if I could have switched to female hormones before all of this damage had been done?

I'm just like many other transgender people: we felt confused about gender as a child, but the lack of information about transgenderism and the resulting social stigma kept most of us from dealing with our gender issues until later in life. As more information has become available, however, the age at which individuals are coming out as transgender has fallen rapidly, and that has led to the development of a very helpful new pre-puberty treatment.

The treatment, described in a report in the 2008 *Journal of Sexual Medicine*, involves administering "gonadotropin-releasing hormone" (GnRH) to delay puberty. The report describes the experience of the VU University clinic in Amsterdam which has, along with clinics in Gent, Boston,

36

Oslo, and Toronto, started to treat or refer for treatment children under the age of sixteen, provided that puberty is at least in its second of five stages. In order to be accepted for treatment, the Amsterdam clinic requires that the child has had Gender Identity Disorder from early childhood, has increased gender dysphoria triggered by puberty, and does not have other psychiatric problems.

One of the obvious reasons for delaying puberty is to allow the individual more time to consider the consequences of transitioning genders before doing so. More importantly, for those who do go on to transition, avoiding puberty spares the torment of watching the "wrong" secondary sex characteristics develop—low voice and male facial features for those who transition to female, and breasts and short stature for those who transition to male—which could cause others to fail to perceive them as a member of their desired gender and possibly to harass or subject them to violence as a result.

Those with extreme cross-gender identification from toddlerhood onward can become depressed, anorexic, or suicidal when the "wrong" secondary sex characteristics start to develop, according to the report. Puberty produces results that cannot be reversed, while the delay of puberty can be stopped at any point without impacting normal pubertal development.

The process is justified, the report claims, because those who later have sex reassignment surgery have better outcomes when the process is started earlier in life. Among other things, not performing the process can cause youth to find illicit sources of hormones and to shun professional health care.

The Amsterdam clinic says it's not unusual these days to have a twelve-year-old applicant accompanied by supportive parents. While the process of delaying puberty is receiving increasing attention and acceptance, it remains difficult to find supportive help for children before they reach the second stage of puberty. This is in part because prevailing research says that symptoms of GID decrease or disappear pre-puberty for 80–95 percent of children, a finding that has traditionally led parents to reject a child's cross-gender feelings or dismiss them as just a phase.

One has to wonder about this research, however, given that the statistic comes in part from the work of Dr. Kenneth Zucker, whose Toronto clinic provides "reparative" treatments that encourage the child to accept their natal sex and associated gender. For example, Zucker orders parents to place a limit on their child's cross-dressing and, for children assigned male at birth, to take away their child's feminine toys, all with the stated goal of reducing the chances that the child will become transsexual. Zucker appears to have a conflict of interest for unbiased research.

Nevertheless, parents these days are more likely than ever to have heard the story of a transgender person or two, and may even have the benefit of having one of us as a friend. The result is that caring parents are now aggressively seeking to help and support their child's intense cross-gender insistence rather than rejecting it as a phase.

Some of these new-age courageous parents were front and center in a special edition of ABC's newsmagazine *20/20* that first aired in 2006 and again with updates in 2007. Barbara Walters devoted the entire hour-long program to three transgender children ages six to twelve (Jazz, Riley, and Jeremy) and to how their parents were coping and helping. ABC supplemented the broadcasts with a very helpful list of resources for parents that continues to be available on its Web site.

But because supporting transgender children is a fairly new phenomenon, other sources of information to help parents are scarce. One promising new book receiving glowing reviews is *The Transgender Child: A Handbook for Families and Professionals* by Stephanie Brill and Rachel Pepper (one of the Ten Books I Recommend in Chapter 28). Brill and Pepper include tips for parents on how to deal with the social, psychological, educational, medical, and legal consequences of being transgender or gender variant. The book includes a foreword by the leading expert in the United States on the care of transgender youth, Dr. Norman Spack of the Gender Management Service clinic of Children's Hospital Boston.

Additional resources will certainly become available in the coming years. This is a good thing, because even when parents are supportive, the child still faces a world that has a way to go before it uniformly embraces transgender children.

10. Discrimination: "Transgender? You're Fired!"

Many Americans do not realize that in much of the country you can be fired just for being transgender. According to the National Center for Transgender Equality, only 37 percent of Americans live in areas that explicitly ban discrimination based on gender identity and expression. For others, legal proceedings may be the only way you can establish your rights. This means that revealing your transgender status could have the same result as that experienced by Sarah Blanchette and Diane Schroer.

Sarah Blanchette was a computer programmer for Saint Anselm College in Manchester, New Hampshire. In March 2004, she informed her superiors that she would return from a two-week vacation presenting herself as female. St. Anselm College then fired her, stating in a letter, "As you know, you recently disclosed to senior college administration your transsexual status. Upon consideration, you are immediately relieved of your duties ... " The Boston-based LGBT advocacy and legal group GLAD (not to be confused with the LGBT national media watchdog GLAAD) filed a lawsuit against Saint Anselm in May 2005, reaching a settlement in December 2006.

Diane Schroer was an Airborne Ranger, a qualified Special Forces officer, who completed more than 450 parachute jumps, received numerous decorations including the Defense Superior Service Medal, and was handpicked to head up a classified national security operation. Shortly after retiring as a colonel after twenty-five years of distinguished service in the army, she accepted a job as a terrorism research analyst at the Library of Congress. Her employer-to-be thought they had found the perfect candidate. But when Schroer told her future supervisor that she was in the process of a gender transition to female, the job offer was rescinded. The American Civil Liberties Union (ACLU) sued, and in September of 2008 a federal judge ruled that the Library of Congress had discriminated against Schroer.

If you are transgender and believe that your industry, employer, or trade will not accept a transgender person, you might decide to leave your current position before disclosing your transgender status. But after disclosure you will likely run into another problem: it can be very difficult to find new employment as an out transgender person, especially if your presentation does not rigidly conform to the gender binary. You may end up settling for employment considerably below your capabilities for the sake of having a job. Or you may not find a job at all.

However rampant and chronic employment discrimination may be for the community, it pales in comparison to the gravest issue facing transgender people: hate crimes. One example was the murder of Gwen Araujo in California in 2002. Gwen was a sexually active teenager who had not disclosed her transgender status to some of her male sex partners. She was murdered by her companions after their forced inspection revealed her to be anatomically male. In the ensuing trial, the defendants tried to use the transgender version of the "gay panic" defense—that Gwen had deceived them and therefore deserved to be murdered. In the end, two of the defendants were convicted of second-degree murder but the jury concluded that no hate crime was committed.

An estimated average of one transgender person every two weeks is murdered just for being transgender. Gwen Smith started the Remembering Our Dead web project in 1999 to memorialize those who were killed due to anti-transgender hatred or prejudice. Out of the project grew the solemn Transgender Day of Remembrance (TDOR), observed each November 20. In 2005, there were 305 TDOR events around the world, spanning forty-two U.S. states and eleven countries on five continents. Ethan St. Pierre now maintains statistics, a list of TDOR locations, and information on those being remembered.

As a trans person you may also face discrimination in your mundane, everyday life in areas such as housing, credit, and public accommodation. If your presentation does not rigidly conform to the gender binary, you may be harassed if you attempt to use either the men's or the ladies' bathroom. Self-deputized gender police (and sometimes, the actual law enforcement kind) stand ready to protect these sacred spaces. The Transgender Law Center's 2005 guide "Peeing in Peace" explains how this policing harms gender-nonconforming people and offers some suggestions to help.

The bathroom situation is further worsened by opponents of transgender rights, who have increasingly claimed that transgender non-discrimination legislation enables sexual predators to dress as women and enter women's bathrooms and locker room facilities. This is highly misleading because the legislation does not alter existing criminal laws against people who commit crimes in bathrooms and locker rooms. Furthermore, there has been no reported increase in criminal activity in restrooms or locker rooms in states or municipalities that have transgender non-discrimination protections in place. Finally, women's groups and those focused on eliminating sexual assault reject the idea that transgender people present any heightened risk to the safety of women and children; they decry the specious characterization of transgender people as predators as diverting attention from the real issues of concern around women's and children's safety.

Regardless of how you present, you may face discrimination just because administrators or employees know you are transgender. GLAD has successfully challenged a situation in which a transgender middle school student was disciplined for wearing gender-appropriate clothing, and another in which a loan applicant was told to go home and come back dressed in clothing that matched the gender on her identification.

Discrimination pops up in all kinds of places, including your tax return. Since you must have the authorization of mental health professionals to have sex-reassignment surgery, and because you must pay the full cost of the surgery given that it is generally not covered by insurance, Rhiannon O'Donnabhain deducted the costs of her sex-reassignment surgery on her 2001 return, believing they surely qualified as medically necessary. Yet, upon audit, the IRS denied her deduction, deeming it cosmetic. GLAD went to trial in U.S. Tax Court in 2007 on her behalf; the decision is still pending.

I have mentioned some of GLAD's transgender legal cases because they are most familiar to me from my position as the first transgender member of its board of directors. But in all fairness, organizations such as Lambda Legal, the National Center for Lesbian Rights, and the Transgender Law Center have also achieved significant legal gains on behalf of trans people. It's clearly going to take the work of all of these organizations and others, plus some significant legislation, before all of us gender-nonconforming people will be able to live our lives in peace.

11. Forced "Out": A Real ID Problem for Transgender People

I started work with a new employer right after transitioning to live as a female in 2002. My previous employer had made it clear that they were not going to accept my gender transition.

It was also the start of my one-year "Real Life Experience" of living in my true gender. RLE, as it's called, is one step in the guidelines for gender transition set by medical professionals. It's intended to serve as a sort of trial one must pass before receiving the medical letter of approval required for sex reassignment surgery. With management at my new job fully aware of the former (male) me, I figured my transgender status might never be an issue.

I quickly filled out the Blue Cross application, excited about the prospect of having health insurance in my new name for the first time. Yet my excitement quickly faded a few days later when Blue Cross called me. "Ms. Herman, there is a person with the same last name in our database who has a male first name. Do you know this person?"

Argh. I had to tell them the truth—I had had Blue Cross coverage as my prior self. "Well, Ms. Herman, we can't code you as female in our system until you've had 'the surgery.'" I tried to explain the hardship that having an M on my HMO card would present. I would have to out myself to every doctor's billing office, explaining that they would need to code me as male in their systems to be sure that their health claims for me were processed.

The representative went off to confer with her underwriting department and then called back. "Sorry, we must code you as male until surgery. And by the way, just a reminder, your surgery will not be covered by insurance." Insult to injury!

My new employer accepted my Social Security card (in my old name), driver's license (old name, gender identity, and picture) and the court's name change order as proof for the I-9 Employment Eligibility Verification form, although they did make it clear that they needed to see my new identification the moment I received it. I was very lucky. Other employers might have declined to employ me until both documents had been changed, a process that can take years.

Not too long after that, I encountered the Social Security Number Verification System. Employers have the option of verifying not only the Social Security number that employees provide, but also the date of birth and gender against the Social Security Administration database. The SSA has gender in their database? Who knew? It doesn't show on the card. Again I was lucky that management knew of my transition.

Around that time, a trans friend who was not out received a call from her employer's human resources department. "Ms. Smith, there's a discrepancy on your employment application that we'd like to discuss." Fortunately, after outing herself they allowed her to keep her job. Other less-aware employers might have fired her—quite legally—for "deception."

I hustled off to the Social Security office with my name-change order in hand. Social Security could change my name, they said, but could not change my gender until I had had genital surgery. Sigh.

My experience at the Department of Motors Vehicles was no better. "I'm sorry, Ms. Herman, we can change your name and your picture, but we cannot change your gender marker without both proof of surgery and a birth certificate showing your new gender. Things have gotten a lot more stringent since 9/11, you know." Me, a potential terrorist? Unbelievable!

I was very lucky to have been born in a different state that issues (upon proof of surgery, of course) a completely new birth certificate showing no trace of the old gender. People born in my current home state can only get an amended birth certificate, which effectively outs them to whoever sees it. Worse, there are some states where one can never, ever change one's birth certificate. Trans people born in those states are stuck with a birth certificate that does not match their gender identity and thus may be stuck with the same discrepancy on other forms of ID issued to agree with the birth certificate.

A few of my transgender friends were able to obtain a driver's license showing their correct gender marker without having had surgery, either because the license was obtained before requirements tightened or because the clerk innocently corrected the gender marker to match the person's presentation. A possible nightmare looms for them, however. That nightmare would be triggered by a new program called Real ID.

The Real ID Act—frequently written in all caps as REAL ID, although it is not an acronym—passed in 2005 as an add-on to a military spending bill. A response to legitimate concerns about terrorists using false identification documents, the act has the effect of standardizing state driver's licenses as a national ID, which means that a more onerous requirement for gender marker changes will be imposed on all fifty states. It also requires that electronic copies of documents used to obtain the license be verified by the state and made available in a federal database unless state policy allows the information to be kept confidential.

For transgender people, this could result in authorities having easy access to evidence of a prior gender and of current surgical status. The Department of Homeland Security (DHS) issued in 2008 its final regulations for implementation of the Real ID Act, and those regulations contain "some significant flaws" for transgender people according to the National Center for Transgender Equality. Deadlines for state compliance run from 2011 through 2017.

Another possible nightmare looms. DHS now requires that employers clear up mismatches with the Social Security Number Verification system in fourteen to sixty days or face charges of having "constructive knowledge" of unauthorized workers on the payroll. Of course, no bureaucracy is guaranteed to work in fourteen to sixty days, so employers may feel forced to fire employees with gender mismatches simply to avoid the risk of penalties.

The National Center for Transgender Equality (NCTE) has useful guidance on what to do if your employer receives a no-match letter and provides the latest information on implementation of the Real ID Act.

When it comes right down to it, all of this fuss is caused by the perceived need to have gender markers on identification documents. But how important is that, really? If the goal is to collect information that identifies the individual, then either the gender marker should be expanded to include not just "male" and "female" but also other possible answers, or it should be removed altogether. As things stands now, it is clearly ineffective and harmful as an identifier for transgender people.

12. Political Correctness: "Please Don't Call Me Tranny"

Just after transition, I attended a social gathering of colleagues from a prior employment. I was certain that the rumor mill had done its job, so I assumed everyone would know about the new me. But I was so wrong—almost no one knew! That was clear after a few greetings. A few people were amazed and welcoming but most were speechless because they just did not know what they could say that would not offend me.

So what is politically correct when speaking with a transgender person? Actually, the rules aren't that different from the rules you follow in talking with anyone else.

First of all, use the pronoun matching the person's appearance. If the person is wearing women's clothing, you'll be safe using "she." But what if the person has not had surgery? Doesn't matter; you should still use "she" if the person is presenting as a woman. Of course, the reverse is true for trans men. Simple so far, right?

But what if the person's appearance does not conform to the gender binary? Trans people are generally happy to have you ask their pronoun preference, because it shows you care. We like your asking much better than if you guess and get it wrong, and we get especially unhappy if you use the pronoun "it." Same rule as for the rest of the population, when you think about it.

For some trans people, the current pair of pronouns just doesn't quite work. Some have gone so far as to propose new ones that are not gender dependent. Far-fetched? Think back a few decades to the height of the second wave of feminism, when the term "Ms." was proposed as a title not dependent on a woman's marital status. It has since grown to be the default title, removing the need to look for the presence or absence of a wedding ring before you speak with a woman.

Title used to be one of the things that needed to be established before a conversation started and gender still is. Why not remove that stress? Trans activist Leslie Feinberg prefers the universal pronoun "ze" and the universal possessive "hir." Personally, I find them a bit awkward, but I felt the same way about "Ms." at the beginning, in large part because it differed from what I was used to. Now I'm glad it's the default.

When you know that a person is transgender, can you ask about hormones and surgery? The answer is the same as it would be for anyone else: no. A person's health history is a private matter, and as is the case for people in other situations, spreading private health information can have adverse consequences for that person. Besides, many trans people don't ever have surgery, for various reasons I've covered in my other chapters.

So what if the trans person volunteers that she/he/ze is on hormones or had surgery? Let the person lead the discussion, as you would non-trans people. Feel free to ask them to explain something further if you don't understand the terminology or procedure. And it's always okay to ask how the person is feeling now.

If I told you that I have had surgery, does that give you permission to ask if my boobs are real or not? Again, the answer is no just like it would be for any other woman. Similarly, you shouldn't ask an FTM "What did you do about your boobs?" Sexual harassment laws protect all people, including those who are transgender.

I've mentioned before that drag kings and queens, cross-dressers, transsexuals, genderqueer people, and intersex people are often included under the transgender umbrella. Should you worry about which of those categories the person falls into? No. Just use the umbrella term transgender, and you'll be politically correct. The person may also tell you which category they prefer.

And be sure to use trans or transgender as an adjective, as one does the word gay. Transgender woman, trans woman, etc. are all okay. But saying, "Joanne is a trans" is not. It's especially offensive to say, "Joanne is a sex change" because that communicates private health information and also is objectifying. For more guidance on terminology and usage, the Media Guide published by Gay and Lesbian Alliance Against Defamation (GLAAD) is quite helpful.

Okay, so you still want to know more about what it means to be transgender, but you've followed my guidelines and your trans friend does not seem open to questions. What do you do now? I have book recommendations for you. See the Ten Books I Recommend in Chapter 28.

Oh, and about the label tranny. It remains a derogatory term, much as queer was for lesbian, gay, and bisexual people not that long ago. Of course, pride about being

L, G, or B has grown, and with that trend, some younger folks have even taking to proudly identifying as queer. A few even prefer the term as being more inclusive than just saying gay, lesbian, or bisexual. Meanwhile, I've noticed a few of my trans friends have on occasion jokingly referred to one another as trannies. Will tranny join the vernacular in the same way queer has? It's too early to tell, so in the meantime, please don't call us tranny.

13. Corporate Acceptance

There was some big news for transgender people in the 2006 Human Rights Campaign Corporate Equality Index (CEI). The annual CEI is a tool to measure how equitably companies are treating their lesbian, gay, bisexual, and transgender (LGBT) employees, consumers, and investors. Scoring 100 percent each year is rapidly becoming essential for major employers.

For 2006, HRC raised the bar to require transgender parity in at least one of five wellness benefits, and the results were exciting. Of the 446 companies in the survey, a total of 303 companies offered at least one of the specified benefits for their transgender employees, and a staggering 67 offered all five. More impressively, 28 percent of the employers provided health benefits for trans-related surgical procedures.

The percentage of employers whose Equal Employment Opportunity policy includes gender identity or expression has grown impressively from 5 percent in 2002 (the first year of the CEI) to 66 percent in the 2009 report. Yet HRC looked more carefully in 2009 at the responses concerning transgender benefits and found, sadly, that only 12 percent of employers surveyed actually provide benefits for transgender surgical procedures.

Dr. Kelley Winters offered a reason for the low number in her 2009 book, *Gender Madness in American Psychiatry: Essays From the Struggle for Dignity* (one of the Ten Books I Recommend in Chapter 28) and expanded on her thinking in her February 2009 *Bilerico*.com post. Because the CEI requires employers to offer only one of its five specified transgender health benefits in order to satisfy the criteria, and because the *DSM IV* diagnoses unfairly favor reparative therapy over transition, employers overwhelmingly choose to offer only mental health benefits.

HRC has responded in a big way. It has announced that the 2012 CEI will require that at least one insurance option available to all employees is a contract where:

A. Transgender exclusions are removed or substantially modified to ensure coverage for transgender-specific treatment either directly in the contract or in clinical guidelines referenced by the contract, and

B. The WPATH Standards of Care are used to determine what treatment will be considered medically necessary and not cosmetic.

This offers the prospect of the first real progress regarding medical coverage. But why the wait? HRC says it needs to give employers time to make the change since benefit plans typically only change once a year and changes need to be in place by June 2011 to make the 2012 CEI. That still feels like one year too long to wait.

HRC says that some companies are surprised to find that their health insurance coverage excludes gender identity-related treatments. The language is often in the master policy because it is the standard offering from the insurance company. Once employers learn this, HRC said it is often only a matter of demanding that their insurers remove the exclusion.

The exclusion is standard because of fears over the cost of inclusion. But Mary Ann Horton, in an eye-opening session at the 2006 Out and Equal Workplace Summit on "The Cost of Transgender Health Benefits," showed convincingly that the cost is considerably less than that of domestic partner coverage, even when taking into account a generous margin of error.

Horton backed up her calculations with the experience of the City and County of San Francisco, which has provided comprehensive transgender health coverage since 2001. Their actuaries knew there were twenty-seven transgender municipal employees, and therefore geared up to pay for thirty-five surgeries each year. But they missed the fact that some transgender people never have surgery and those that do generally only have it once in a lifetime. Actual cost experience has been no worse than that for gall bladder removal or heart surgery.

In 2005, Raytheon made history when it became the first of the major aerospace and defense contractors to add gender identity and expression to its employment nondiscrimination policy, a requirement to score 100 percent on the CEI. In 2006, Raytheon was joined at 100 percent by three of their competitors. Clearly, there is a domino effect going on out there. Raytheon upped the ante by announcing at the 2006 Out and Equal Summit that they would be the first corporate sponsor of the Southern Comfort Conference, probably the largest transgender conference in the U.S.

The Out and Equal Summit has a lot of programming on other topics of interest to corporate LGBT employee resource groups, but transgender inclusion was a definite theme in 2006. The theme was set in the opening plenary by the head of GlaxoSmithKline's HIV-related business and the doctor who discovered AZT, each expressing their own heartfelt pride that GSK had just added gender identity and expression to its nondiscrimination policy. Neither stumbled once when talking about the importance of transgender inclusion, as others do when giving it lip service. GSK clearly showed it gets it.

Trans inclusion in the workplace was one of the topics covered by a panel of executive directors from national LGBT organizations. Mara Keisling, executive director of the National Center for Transgender Equality, sat on the panel as an equal with Neil Giuliano of GLAAD, Kate Kendell of National Center for Lesbian Rights , and Alexander Robinson of the National Black Justice Coalition. It was very clear from their remarks that all were collaborating around inclusion.

Another well-attended feature session, sponsored by Intel, featured Andrea James and Calpernia Addams discussing their experience as consultants for the production of the movie *Transamerica*. They spoke about their efforts to change Hollywood's portrayal of trans people, a key step toward acceptance by Americans at large. Other sessions covered corporate transition guidelines as well as training for those who wish to do transgender-inclusion training in their companies.

But I was most struck by a session led by Dr. Louise Young, the Raytheon senior software engineer and self-described "longtime lesbian activist" who founded the Raytheon GLBTA employee resource group. Louise explained the evolution of her understanding of transgender: her realization that trans people are very much part of the LGBT community, her spearheading of Raytheon's efforts to add gender identity and expression to the EEO policy, and finally her pride in serving recently as the subject matter expert for a Raytheon division wanting to understand a colleague's impending transition from male to female.

Louise Young is not transgender, but she is a capital A trans ally. She was not the only one at the summit. I met several non-transgender corporate representatives who genuinely wanted to embrace transgender people at their companies and realized that they needed to understand us in order to do so. Attendees were full of questions for all of the trans presenters at the summit—and even for me, just another attendee. It's clear that corporate America is starting to get the "T." How is your company doing?

14. Transgender Success Stories

I might have transitioned sooner to live as a female had there been greater public awareness of transgender people. There has been no shortage of stereotypes and Hollywood images, but none of them ever seemed to fit me. It wasn't until I read *Crossing*, the autobiography of noted economist and university professor Deirdre McCloskey, that I started to realize that there are transgender people in every walk of life—even mine.

Since then I have learned of lots of transgender success stories, many of which were not widely known because those involved had kept quiet about their transgender status. I'd like to share some of those stories with you. Since my space is limited, I'm going to limit this chapter to stories you probably have not heard. That means I'll only mention people outside of the entertainment industry and those whose day jobs do not directly involve transgender activism.

One of the more famous success stories in this category is that of computer scientist Prof. Lynn Conway. Lynn invented technology while she was at IBM in the 1960s that is used in most computers today. But when Lynn announced her plans to transition from male to female, she was fired. How ironic that seems now because the IBM of today was the first corporation to add gender identity and expression to its global nondiscrimination policy.

Following her transition in 1968, Lynn chose to live stealth (without disclosing transgender status, as explained in Chapter 5) to preserve her career prospects. She went on to a distinguished research career, pioneering new methods of computer chip design while working at Xerox's legendary Palo Alto, California research laboratory, and she is now professor emerita of engineering at the University of Michigan and a prestigious Fellow of the IEEE. She chose to come out as transgender only in 1999, when an author writing on the history of computer science set out to find the person who had developed that amazing technology at IBM.

Since then, Lynn has devoted much time to making information about transgenderism available in as many languages as possible. I probably would not have had the courage to transition if it weren't for her profiles of successful transitioners on her Web site.

There are other transgender successes in academia. Ben Barres is a popular professor of neurobiology at Stanford who made headlines when his article challenging sexist comments made by former Harvard president Lawrence Summers was published in the prestigious scientific journal *Nature*. My hat is off to Ben. He has seen firsthand, through his transition from female just how much bias there is facing women who pursue careers in the sciences. I applaud him for speaking out against this bias as a man.

There are transgender successes in everyday politics too. Computer specialist and Air Force veteran Jessica Orsini was elected to the Centralia, Missouri board of aldermen.

Raytheon Missile Systems chief engineer Amanda Simpson made history as the first openly transgender candidate nominated for state office by a political party. She narrowly missed winning a seat in the Arizona House of Representatives in 2004. And retired surgeon Dana Beyer snagged the endorsement of political powerhouses The Victory Fund and Emily's List in her 2006 bid to be the first transgender member of the Maryland House of Delegates.

You can even find successful transgender people among ordained clergy. In 1996 the Reverend Erin Swenson became the first known mainstream Protestant minister to make an open gender transition while remaining in ordained office. She is currently serving at the Ormewood Park and Morningside Presbyterian Churches in Atlanta. And the Reverend Malcolm Himschoot was ordained by the United Church of Christ as an openly transgender man at age twenty-seven and went on to serve as associate minister at the Plymouth Congregational Church in Minneapolis, a congregation with 1,800 members.

In the corporate world, Melissa Feinmel is one of at least five transgender pilots flying for American Airlines, Margaret Stumpp manages billions of dollars of investments for Prudential Financial, and Meghan Stabler is a global marketing executive for corporate software giant BMC Software. All have received leading-edge support from their employers or clients.

There are many more transgender success stories, but you rarely hear of them because of the media's fondness for sensationalized stories and depictions of the downtrodden. You may even have a transgender success story working next to you but don't know it because the person is afraid that being out may cost him or her their job. Hopefully, as transgender awareness increases, the stigma of being transgender will decrease, the laws will improve, and transgender people will feel freer to be out of the closet.

As for me? I'm just the financial controller for a very supportive arts foundation, but the true measure of my success may not come until we see how well this book sells ...

ADVANCED TOPICS

15. Gender Transition Regret

With the release of Renée Richards' most recent book, *No Way Renée: The Second Half of My Notorious Life*, the topic of gender transition regret again came out of the closet. Her book was primarily the story of her family, career, tennis, and social life. Yet in a pre-release interview with *The New York Times*, the reporter asked Richards if she regretted having had sex-reassignment surgery. Even though Richards said no, the headline was "The Lady Regrets." Why is there such curiosity about whether transitioners regret their transitions?

Many transgender people actually do not undergo a gender transition. But a transsexual person feels so strongly about having a gender identity at odds with his or her anatomy that he or she may seek a medical intervention or physical change. Some transsexual people do not need sex-reassignment surgery (SRS) to resolve the incongruity, while others desire it but cannot afford it.

Lynn Conway, renowned professor emerita at the University of Michigan, estimates that one in 2,500 U.S. citizens has undergone male-to-female SRS (there is no contemporary statistic available for female-to-male SRS).

As one who is included in Conway's statistic, I am used to fielding the question about regret. Societal taboos about crossing the gender binary make any transition seem remarkable, and so the fact that someone made a seemingly permanent change (i.e., surgery) and might have regretted it is positively tabloid news. (By the way, I don't regret mine.)

But how often does it happen that someone regrets having had SRS? Research has been scarce because of the stigma associated with studying transgenderism and because most of the necessary subjects (transsexual individuals) have been highly closeted until recent times. The only contemporary research I could find, a 2002 paper in the *International Journal of Transgenderism* citing a 1992 study, observed that "the incidence of postoperative regret is generally extremely low ... less than 1 percent in female-to-males and 1–1.5 percent in male-to-females."

A 2007 study by the University Hospitals of Leicester in the UK measured satisfaction with surgery results (MTF only) rather than SRS-regret. Of the 222 male-to-female participants aged nineteen to seventy-six, 88 percent were happy with the surgery at their first visit. Of the seventy contacted three years later for detailed follow-up, 80 percent said the surgery had met expectations. Most problems identified were relatively minor and easily corrected by secondary surgery.

The regret numbers are pretty low. Why the concern?

Some may view it as an unmitigated disaster that anyone—even one single person—had his penis "cut off" or her breasts removed and then regretted it. Because of this, trans people must undergo one of the most rigorous evaluations of any medical procedure in order to qualify for SRS. This evaluation, unfortunately, favors those who can best convince the system of their need; thereby it occasionally disqualifies some who need the surgery while qualifying some who don't.

Others may reject the regret statistics as being improbably low. If a story of one person's regrets makes the headlines, you worry that there must be other stories, right? You may even know a transgender person who is unhappy about some aspect of his or her life and assume that aspect is their surgery.

But the worriers need to look at the big picture. Any gender transition, whether it involves surgery or not, is a major life change. It impacts details of your daily life far beyond the wearing of a different wardrobe, especially if it includes the loss of ties to loved ones, loss of work, or the need to move. Transgender people respond to any major change just like the population at large does. Some navigate change with incredible resilience, many have their ups and downs, and a few are positively consumed by it.

Transitioning also makes you a member of a minority group, perhaps for the first time. Like racial and ethnic minorities, transgender people often cannot hide their "uniqueness" and as a result can face discrimination in employment, housing, education, and public accommodation. Of course, if you are a transgender person and a member of a racial or ethnic minority, expect your challenges to be compounded.

You also have a problem unique to the LGBT (lesbian, gay, bisexual or transgender) minority group. That is, few (if any) members of your family share your minority status. In a racial or ethnic minority at least the family stands with you as a minority. As an LGBT individual, family solidarity is not assured. In fact, one or more family members may even become the most ardent opponent(s) of your transition, out of supposed love and concern for you.

There are also challenges unique to a gender transition. For male-to-female, it can be frustrating to experience the loss of male privilege. I'm also guessing that Renée Richards's brash personality probably played better in her former life. For female-to-male, it may be disheartening to see how women you don't know now avoid your glance and keep their distance from you. Transitioners in either direction may find sexual intimacy more elusive.

Finally, there are challenges specific to hormone therapy and surgery. Medical surveillance is essential. But it's often not easy to find care that is both transgender-aware and welcoming. And if you do find suitable transgender health care, you may have trouble affording it because insurance generally does not cover it.

In spite of all of these challenges, most people who transition genders remain resolved that living in one's perceived gender is an imperative, not a choice. Many will have regrets about the consequences of their transition, but few will regret the transition itself. In the unusual case where the consequences were overwhelming enough to prompt a de-transition, the return to the old gender is seldom satisfactory either.

Sadly, many of these consequences are the direct result of the lack of awareness of and misconceptions of transgender people by friends, families, colleagues, and others—misconceptions that led to Largo, Florida's vote to dismiss a longtime and capable city manager before she had even started her transition to female. Shameful stories show that a lot of people need to read this book.

16. Is It Deception or Just Being Prudent?

The *St. Petersburg Times* reported that Largo, Florida city manager Steve (now Susan) Stanton, who lost her job in February of 2007, and a Largo city commissioner who voted for Stanton's dismissal, had attended the same National League of Cities conference in March 2006. The *Times* disclosed that Stanton attended at least two of the seminars dressed as a woman, and the commissioner was not aware that the woman in those seminars was Stanton. The commissioner was quoted as saying he was disturbed that Stanton "misrepresented himself (sic) on the city's dime" and that this behavior was one reason he "no longer trust[ed] Stanton to run Largo City Hall."

Ah, yes. For those who feel that being transgender is a bad thing, having been in close proximity to a transgender person without realizing it is even worse—as if it should have been obvious that a person is transgender. So when it's *not* obvious, the trans person gets accused of willful deception. Thank goodness Stanton's only punishment was dismissal from her job. California teenager Gwen Araujo was brutally murdered in 2002 when her lovers discovered she was trans.

Stanton was actually dealing prudently with one of the challenges faced by those who transition to female after several years living as a male. For better or worse, society expects women her age to behave a certain way, especially women in public positions. How do you acquire these social skills without the benefit of the socialization most girls experience in their teens?

What Stanton did is fairly common. Most therapists (remember—it's very difficult to transition genders under the generally accepted treatment standards without professional supervision) recommend some period of part-time presentation prior to transition. Their first recommendation is often to meet others like yourself at the local transgender social group, if there is one, or at a regional transgender conference if you can afford it.

But eventually you need experience being a woman in the "real world" before facing those who know you. In my case, the best I could do before transition was to visit a large shopping mall outside Boston once a week presenting as Joanne. I was able to make purchases thanks to a second credit card in my current name that I had added to an existing account. That experience of transacting with others definitely allowed me to assimilate more easily when I transitioned.

But Stanton, a public servant facing far more scrutiny than I did, had an opportunity to be Susan at a business conference. By taking advantage of it, she received valuable real-world experience away from almost all the people who know her.

Would the commissioner have accepted Stanton's action if he had been prepared ahead of time? I doubt it. Society still suffers from what I call MIDS—Man in a Dress Syndrome. We have largely accepted women in the workplace, but when men put on the clothes of women they are immediately presumed less capable. Could this be one of the reasons that working women as a whole still earn less than men? Feels to me like evidence that the patriarchy lives on (see Chapter 19 for more evidence).

Some others who did not know of the seminar episode accused Stanton of willfully hiding her transgender status while on the job as Steve. One citizen said, "I don't think we should be paying him (sic) $150,000 a year when he's (sic) not been truthful." Another said, "The issue is not the gender change here ... it's that he (sic) deceived people."

About what? Stanton admitted in another *Times* story that she had gone through periods of cross-dressing in private before reaching her decision to transition. Cross-dressing is also something not uncommon among male-to-female transitioners prior to transition. But women have been wearing male-like suits for years, ever since that was a prerequisite for corporate advancement in the 1970s. Are the objectors saying that men can't dress in a female way even in private? Seems like further evidence that feminine appearance is discounted.

Then there were those who objected to not knowing sooner about Stanton's transition plans. The *Times* says that Stanton came out to another commissioner, the fire chief, the police chief, and the mayor in the year preceding her dismissal. She knew her news would be controversial, and so she did what any good manager would do—built support so that others would more easily accept the change and so the city would continue to function smoothly.

She was wise to do so: witness the circus that followed the unplanned early release of her news to the general public, costing her her job.

The *St. Petersburg Times* provided comprehensive coverage of the Stanton firing, including Howard Troxler's excellent commentary "Stones Fly in Largo; Society Is Thus Saved," which highlighted the religious hypocrisy in some of the comments at the hearing where Stanton was dismissed.

Transgender status remains headline news, and it bears noting that it was the *St. Petersburg Times* that outed Stanton in the first place. Editor Diane Steinle admitted so in a story, denying the claim of a local church that the *Times* was somehow "in cahoots" with Stanton about her plans. Steinle said that when she heard the news, she immediately "called Stanton and refused to grant him (sic) an off-the-record interview ... a public figure's planning to get a sex change certainly was important news."

"Certainly"? God forbid anyone be deceived about a person's gender!

17. Religion and Transgender People

With dozens of citizens speaking at the February 2007 hearing that ultimately led to the dismissal of Susan Stanton, then city manager of Largo, Florida, the media needed a pithy sound bite. It got an especially good one: "If Jesus was here tonight—and believe me, I know the Bible—I can guarantee you he'd want [Stanton] terminated." Those words were spoken by the Reverend Ron Sanders, pastor for the Lighthouse Baptist Church. Never mind that his church has only thirty members; his words were broadcast around the world. Why? Because we (or at least the media) tend to assume that any one clergyperson may speak for all religious people.

Meanwhile, in an interesting coincidence, *Newsweek* ran a story around the same time about Boston University professor Stephen Prothero's 2007 book *Religious Literacy*. A prime tenet of Prothero's book is that while more than 90 percent of Americans say they believe in God, only a tiny portion actually knows anything about religion. *Newsweek* says that almost everyone fails Prothero's religious literacy quiz on the basics such as the names of the four Gospels. (You'll find a link to his quiz on his Web site.)

If Prothero's assertion is correct, many Americans must be relying on others to interpret religious tenets and, even worse, may be unable to recognize when clergy are embellishing a bit—to put it politely. As one of the citizens at the Largo hearing said, "I wanted to quote the story of Jesus leading the mob to come take someone's job, but I couldn't find that passage in the Bible."

Of course, transgender people definitely encounter problem passages in the Bible. Deuteronomy 22:5 says, "The woman shall not wear that which pertaineth unto a man, neither shall a man put on a woman's garment: for all that do are an abomination unto the Lord thy God." Deuteronomy 23:1 says, "No one whose testicles are crushed or whose penis is cut off shall be admitted to the assembly of the Lord."

But as Justin Tanis, an ordained minister who is also a program manager for the National Center for Transgender Equality, pointed out in a 2006 interview for the *Washington Blade*, "Deuteronomy also forbids eating shellfish, mixing seed in a field, or blending fabrics."

In fact, if all of the rules of the Bible were strictly enforced, folks would be put to death for working on the Sabbath (Exodus 35:2) and stoned for using the Lord's name in vain (Leviticus 24:16). Furthermore, any person with a handicap or any sort of blemish would be forbidden to approach the altar (Leviticus 21).

Meanwhile, biologist Joan Roughgarden noted that the Bible actually provides evidence that transgender people were a part of regular life even in biblical times. Roughgarden is a transgender woman who has taught at Stanford University since 1972.

Roughgarden is also a Christian who has done extensive reading of the Bible. In her book, *Evolution and Christian Faith*, she offers the radical notion that the two beliefs are actually quite compatible. She claims that Jesus's beliefs and teachings actually were intended to help Christians live with the diversity that existed then and that would continue to be present.

Of relevance to trans people is her discussion of eunuchs. She references Matthew 19:12, in which Jesus describes three types of eunuchs—those "which were so born from their mothers' womb," those "which were made eunuchs of men," and those "which made themselves eunuchs for the kingdom of heaven's sake."

Roughgarden interprets the first category as describing intersex individuals and the latter transsexual individuals. She notes that Jesus' descriptions line up with those of ancient Roman writers who described those we would today call cross-dressers as well as those who transitioned genders without physical alteration.

She points out that some eunuchs held powerful positions and that "eunuchs were common enough that writers referred to them with such phrases as 'armies of eunuchs.'" And she asserts that the apostle Philip's baptism of the eunuch in Acts 9:27–38 serves as an "explicit instruction to include eunuchs within the church."

But statements at the Largo hearing implied otherwise. If Americans are truly as biblically illiterate as Stephen Prothero asserts, rhetoric like Pastor Ron's can and does end up being taken as gospel.

Many LGBT people have been hurt by religion used in hate, and transgender people are no exception. I nervously returned to church only when my late wife, Barbara, was dying of cancer, and I needed a spiritual connection during those difficult days. What I discovered was that there are progressive mainline churches that truly welcome LGBT folks, and their leaders are convinced that Jesus would (and did) too. You can read my faith story in Chapter 24.

So don't hesitate to question sweeping generalizations about Jesus. If you are a Christian, please do your own research. Help show Pastor Ron that his is not the last word on transgender people.

18. Transgender People on the Small Screen

In the 2006–2007 season, we saw transgender characters in recurring roles on popular television programs for the first time, instead of one-episode, single-season cameos. In prime time, viewers of the popular ABC sitcom *Ugly Betty* saw the return of Alex Meade as Alexis (played by actress Rebecca Romijn). And during the day, viewers of ABC's long-running soap *All My Children* witnessed Zoe (played by actor Jeffrey Carlson) deal with her transition to female.

ABC was very careful to seek the guidance of media watchdog GLAAD about Zoe's character and chose to cast a male actor for the role, resulting in a very realistic and perhaps even overly sensitive portrayal. And while *Ugly Betty*'s story line does not lend itself to educating the public about transgenderism, Alexis has managed to avoid many of the stereotypes and sensationalism that have characterized transgender roles in the past.

I suppose we can forgive the casting of the gorgeous Romijn as Hollywood's idea of a trans woman, in much the same way lesbians watched *The L Word* in spite of its slick L.A. lesbian chic. I have to admit I had fun imagining myself in Zoe's place as she fell in love with the very cute Bianca (played by actress Eden Riegel), the lesbian character known for participating in the first romantic kiss between two women on a daytime soap opera (*All My Children* in 2003).

Previously, the closest we had come to a recurring transgender character was on the CBS show *The Education of Max Bickford* in 2001. Actress Helen Shaver (of *Desert Hearts* fame) played Erica Bettis, a forty-something professor at an all-female college who had just returned to work after her sex-reassignment surgery. While Shaver played the part very realistically and her character dealt sensitively with some real-life transgender issues, Erica quietly disappeared from the show after only a few episodes. Some say that was the beginning of the end for the series, which was canceled only a few weeks later.

Of course, all of these television transgender roles have been played by non-transgender actors and actresses. But here we have a milestone too: the 2006–2007 season saw trans actress Candis Cayne as a murder victim in the episode "The Lying Game" on the hit CBS series *CSI: New York*. Her role, too, was a step up for the *CSI* series, in which transgender characters central to the plot have previously appeared only as murderers—Paul Millander in 2002 and Dr. Lavalle in 2004. (Some transgender people did have ancillary non-criminal roles in that 2004 episode.)

In spite of that progress, *CSI* still has a long way to go. Cayne's character was a confusion of transgender types. She clearly presented as a woman and yet was shown using the men's room, probably because the writers thought that's what we do when we have not had sex-reassignment surgery. Even though there was nothing about her character that felt like a gay man in drag, the murderer responded with the "ick factor" over the thought that he kissed a guy, which offended many gay, lesbian, or bisexual viewers in the process. And when the victim's body was discovered, the detective declared that "Jane Doe is actually a John," as if all transgender people are involved in sex work. Even the episode's title was a slur against trans people who have not had surgery.

On the serious side, there was a huge milestone achieved in the 2006–2007 season thanks to the ABC newsmagazine *20/20*. Barbara Walters devoted an entire program to an informed and sensitive look at the issues of transgender children. For many viewers, it was their first exposure to trans kids and—more significantly—an introduction to amazing parents who understand their child's gender non-conformance rather than rejecting it. ABC posted additional helpful information on its Web site, including a comprehensive list of resources for parents, which remains available, along with the stories of the children profiled.

But as good as that *20/20* episode was, the 2006–2007 season also included one of the worst televised documentaries ever. MSNBC's *Born in the Wrong Body* set a new low for the portrayal of transgender women. Virtually every camera shot seemed to be of a trans woman putting on lipstick or pantyhose, as if that's the overriding reason someone would transition to female. This is yet another example of the sexism we trans women are subjected to, as I expand on in Chapter 19.

It's too bad, because the MSNBC documentary also featured some very insightful and useful segments from an interview with Simon Aronoff, deputy director of the National Center for Transgender Equality at the time.

Arnoff's Trans Media Watch blog highlighted another problem we had in the 2006–2007 season—the f word. No, not the one you were thinking of. Transgender people have an additional f word: freak. Radio talk show host

Michael Savage used it in reference to murder victim Ruby Ordenana, as if transgenderism justified her murder. Okay, so Savage's show is not on TV, but his rant did make nightly news broadcasts.

Glenn Beck of CNN (now of Fox News) has used the f word in the past, and Tucker Carlson of MSNBC has come oh so close. Even mild-mannered movie critic David Edelstein used it on the CBS *Sunday Morning* program when referring to trans characters in *Hairspray* and *Hedwig and the Angry Inch*.

In spite of these glaring problems, the 2006–2007 television season clearly built on the strength of two breakthroughs from the year before: *Transamerica*, the popular big-screen feature starring Felicity Huffman, and *TransGeneration*, the Sundance Channel series about four transgender college kids. But while we may have moved up from murderer to victim on *CSI*, I have a feeling the writers are unlikely to make any of us the star detectives any time soon.

Update: Another First

From 2007 to 2008, Cadnis Cayne played Carmelita Rainer, a trans woman having an affair with married New York Attorney General Patrick Darling (played by William Baldwin), on the ABC prime time drama *Dirty Sexy Money*. According to Wikipedia, the role made Cayne the first transgender actor to play a recurring transgender character in prime time.

19. Sexism and Transgender People

Transsexuals, who live or seek to live as the gender opposite the one assigned at birth, and who may utilize hormones and surgery to help do so, represent only part of the large and diverse transgender community. I am a male-to-female (MTF) transsexual. J. Michael Bailey, the psychologist who authored the controversial 2003 book *The Man Who Would Be Queen: The Science of Gender-Bending and Transsexualism*, is not.

Bailey concluded, based largely on interviews with transsexuals in a gay bar, that MTF transsexuals transition solely to satisfy their sex drive. Bailey claimed that some of us are really gay men who believe that being a woman will normalize our attraction to men, that some of us are men sexually aroused by the idea of having a female body, and that the rest of us are lying when we say we don't fit those two categories. Noticeably absent in his book is a discussion of female-to-male (FTM) transsexuals.

I (and most other MTF transsexuals) feel strongly that we don't fit Bailey's two categories. We are furious at being called liars by a non-transgender "expert." While most trans people were deeply closeted in years past, that's no longer the case. So the backlash by trans activists in 2003, when his book came out, was intense.

That backlash was rekindled in 2007 on word that another non-transgender "expert," Alice Dreger, was about to publish an article in the *Archives of Sexual Behavior* asserting that the personal attacks on Bailey by trans activists presented "problems not only for science but free expression itself."

As reported by Prof. Lynn Conway on her Web site, Dreger went on to attempt to quash a panel proposed by transgender graduate student and Point Foundation Scholar Joelle Ruby Ryan, defaming her in the process. The panel for the June 2008 National Women's Studies Association Conference was entitled: "The Bailey Brouhaha: Community Members Speak Out on Resisting Transphobia and Sexism in Academia and Beyond." It was held as scheduled, nonetheless, providing the first-ever academic forum for our views. Joelle is now a PhD.

Dreger's defense sounds very much like the rhetoric of non-gay psychiatrist Charles Socarides after he ended up on the wrong side of the vote to remove homosexuality from the American Psychiatric Association's *Diagnostic and Statistical Manual of Mental Disorders* in the early 1970s. Socarides felt the APA's decision was not based on any empirical evidence but influenced by gays, from both within and outside the organization, who had their own agenda.

Focusing on the loud criticisms of Bailey is like discussing the clashes between protesters and police in Chicago at the 1968 Democratic National Convention without recognizing the incredible wave of social change sweeping the nation at the time. Trans people have reached the point that they are fed up with any non-trans "expert"—not just Bailey—who dismisses our opinions. Our view is that, much like a non-gay person can't possibly imagine loving someone of the same sex, a non-transgender person can't possibly imagine the feeling of living in the wrong gender.

Trans people are venting years of frustration. Julia Serano wrote a crisp summary of the Bailey developments on the *Feministing* blog. But more importantly, this rising star's new book, *Whipping Girl: A Transsexual Woman on Sexism and the Scapegoating of Femininity* (one of the Ten Books I Recommend in Chapter 28), has shed much-needed light on the bigger picture.

She starts with the observation that MTF transsexuals pose a problem for the patriarchy. We actually prefer to be female and jump through a huge number of hoops to get there. This very fact subverts the idea of male superiority: how can anyone possibly believe that male is not better? On the other hand, FTM transsexuals transition in the "right" direction, so the patriarchy rarely conducts research about them.

As treatment started becoming available in this country in the 1970s, the non-transgender men running the gender clinics set the femininity requirement very high to limit the number the number of "subversives" admitted. Some clinics even limited treatment, reserving it for MTFs who aroused the male doctor sexually, thereby objectifying them as sex objects.

When non-transgender second-wave feminists saw these über-feminine products of the clinics, they assumed that no thinking person could willingly choose to so actively embrace that level of femininity. They labeled us as dupes of the patriarchy deployed to preserve feminine stereotypes. In reality, we knew full well what we were doing—we were embracing excessive femininity because it was the only way to access the treatment that would allow us to live in our perceived gender.

Even gay male activists of the time reacted with the view espoused by Jim Fouratt that MTF transsexuals were just misguided men who love men and undergo "painful physical body manipulation and dangerous hormonal injects (sic) ... in order to be accepted into heterosexual society."

Treatment standards today are set by the largely male, largely non-transgender World Professional Association for Transgender Health. The standards may have softened a bit because of some transgender input, but they nonetheless remain some of the most rigorous prequalification guidelines of any medical condition. (I describe the current standards and the problems caused by them in Chapter 6).

Of course, the largely male-run insurance industry does its part to limit the number of "subversives" by excluding transgender health coverage from most private insurance. And the IRS sets limits too by challenging in federal tax court in Boston a trans woman's deduction for sex-reassignment surgery, an expense she incurred because her insurance did not cover it despite her meeting the WPATH standards. (The court has not yet ruled in this case.)

It's not just transgender activists who have raised concerns. According to trans blogger Autumn Sandeen in a post on *Pam's House Blend*, noted gender therapist Sandra Samons has voiced to other WPATH members her objection to Bailey's implication "that any therapists who did not agree with him had been duped by transgender people."

Accused of lying, treated as sex objects, labeled dupes and dupers, subjected to excessive pretreatment requirements, denied insurance, and denied our voice—is it any wonder that transsexuals are upset? Even the rest of the transgender community—the part that is not transsexual—gets on our case from time to time for all of the attention we attract for issues that are not theirs.

Bailey and his non-transgender cronies should have realized the risk in offending such a long-oppressed group. His book appeared when we had reached our last straw. In the words of Howard Beale in the 1976 movie *Network*, we're now "mad as hell and ... not going to take this anymore!"

20. Feminism and Transgender People

Janice Raymond is a non-transgender lesbian feminist who was a professor of women's studies at Hampshire College when she wrote the 1979 book *Transsexual Empire: The Making of the She-male*. In her book Raymond completely dismissed the notion that an individual could have a valid belief of being a different gender from the one assigned at birth. And with that as a foundation, *Empire* advanced the following two stereotypes:

(1) Male-to-female transsexuals are merely male agents of the patriarchy who are reinforcing feminine stereotypes. MTF lesbian feminists are really men masquerading as women so they can invade and dominate women's space.

(2) Female-to-male transsexuals are merely women who have copped out of the women's movement by changing themselves rather than changing society.

The first stereotype is no doubt one reason why the long-running Michigan Womyn's Music Festival maintains a policy, reiterated in 2006, of limiting the festival to "womyn-born-womyn." The second stereotype, say detractors, is perpetuated in director Catherine Crouch's *The Gendercator*, the short film pulled from the 2007 San Francisco LGBT film festival Frameline after the trans community raised concerns.

Raymond based her book on what was known about transsexualism at the time, which was not much. *Empire* gave the appearance of providing well-researched insights into a much-unknown population. Her book became part of women's studies curricula and was widely available at feminist booksellers. Because no counterbalancing works had been (or could be) published for years, a whole generation of women has an understanding of transsexuals that's been influenced by Raymond's thinking.

But much has changed since *Empire* was written.

(1) As depicted in the movie *If These Walls Could Talk 2*, lesbian feminists in the 1970s found themselves excluded from feminist groups because, as the character Diane puts it, it was "too risky to take on your issues right now." It makes sense that Raymond might therefore have viewed transsexual lesbian feminists as inhibiting acceptance of lesbian feminists by the wider feminist community. Fortunately, postmodern feminists are taking a more inclusive view.

(2) Raymond was alarmed by the opening of more than twenty university gender clinics in the 1970s. She saw this growing "medical conglomerate," which united medical specialties under one roof to "create" transsexuals, as the patriarchy's "transsexual empire." However, as trans woman Dallas Denny explained in *Transgender Tapestry* magazine, the clinics spouted up because treatment until then had been largely unavailable in this country. Most of the university gender clinics had disappeared by the time Denny wrote her piece in 1991, and services today are

provided mostly by unaffiliated professionals. So much for the empire.

(3) *Empire* was correct in asserting that gender clinics reinforced gender-role stereotypes. At the time, overwhelmingly male legislatures had made it a crime in many states to impersonate a female. Limiting treatment to those who passed in their perceived gender allowed these small clinics to deal with the overwhelming demand and, conveniently, increased the likelihood that society would deem the outcome positive. But access to treatment today is gated much more by an ability to pay, as treatment is usually not covered by insurance. Surely the patriarchy would overcome this financial roadblock if it were truly out to create an empire of transsexuals.

(4) Raymond grounded her thinking in part on the research of Johns Hopkins University psychologist John Money. In the 1972 college textbook *Man & Woman, Boy & Girl*, which he wrote with current Columbia medical psychology professor Anke A. Ehrhardt, he asserted that social factors lock in a child's gender identity in the first eighteen months of life. But this assertion has in recent years been challenged, since some babies born with ambiguous genitalia—some of whom have been surgically "made" female at birth and rigidly raised as girls—choose later to transition to male in order to respond to a strongly held male identity. These cases (which included Money's own star patient) coupled with other new research have led to the current thinking that gender identity is likely set in the womb.

(5) Raymond revealed that she had spoken with only fifteen transsexuals, of whom "several" were prostitutes. Because all transgender academics at the time were deeply closeted for fear of losing their jobs, we had no voice to

challenge Raymond's research. Today, things are different. When J. Michael Bailey released his 2003 book *The Man Who Would Be Queen*, based largely on interviews of transsexuals in a gay bar, a number of out trans academics quickly banded together to denounce his sex-obsessed findings and lack of research. Bailey subsequently resigned as chairman of Northwestern University's psychology department.

(6) When *Empire* was written, the oppression that transgender people suffer at the hands of the patriarchy was not yet visible. In the 2006 report "50 Under 30: Masculinity and the War on America's Youth," the Gender Public Advocacy Coalition (GenderPAC) revealed that 92 percent of victims of gender-based violence were biologically male but presenting with some degree of femininity. In cases where the assailant was known, he was always male. Transgender people are clearly not agents of the patriarchy; we are its victims too.

Interestingly, Raymond and the other feminists who have taken transgender people to task over the years have aimed their critiques almost exclusively at male-to-female transsexuals. In her approachable and thought-provoking 2007 book *Whipping Girl: A Transsexual Woman on Sexism and the Scapegoating of Femininity* (one of the Ten Books I Recommend in Chapter 28), biologist and transsexual lesbian feminist Julia Serano aptly labels this bias "trans-misogyny." Finally, we have an academic work with the standing to challenge Raymond and get to the heart of the issue.

But really, why do Raymond's offensive stereotypes about transsexuals persist when history has largely absolved us from our accused roles as accomplices of the patriarchy? The irony seems to be that in seeking to eradicate gender-role stereotypes, Janice Raymond actually perpetuated two more.

21. Transgender People and LGBT Board Involvement

Late in 2006, the media reported that ABC was adding a transgender character to its long-running daytime soap *All My Children (AMC)*. Most of the articles I read carefully pointed out that the network had prudently sought the advice of LGBT media watchdog GLAAD in advance of introducing Zarf/Zoe.

Ironically, at about the same time, I received at home a fundraising letter from GLAAD. After initially using the term LGBT, the letter spoke only of the concerns of gay people. But not all transgender people are gay. I'm sure GLAAD's letter would have been worded more inclusively if they had at least one transgender person on their board. So why didn't they?

To be fair, GLAAD did have some fine transgender *employees* at that point—I knew two of them personally. And, judging by the *AMC* episodes, it seemed that they had given excellent advice to ABC. Also, GLAAD did name Donna Rose to its board a few weeks after this column was first published in 2006.

GLAAD was not alone in its omission of transgender people. The 2006 survey of the Movement Advancement Project found that there were only nineteen transgender people among the 541 total members of the boards of the top twenty-six LGBT organizations. The study concluded that, while the proportion "may be reasonable" versus the population as a whole, it "may be low considering that the organizations aspire to serve transgender people as well." Other major LGBT organizations reporting no trans board members in 2006 included GLSEN, Lambda Legal, and NCLR.

MAP's 2008 report showed only a slight improvement: it found fifty-five transgender people among the 890 total members of the boards of the top fifty-two LGBT organizations, a little over 6 percent. But by relating recent data on transgender prevalence (1.5 percent: see Chapter 4) and gay/lesbian prevalence (4.1 percent according to the Williams Institute), it is clear that this percentage would need to be 37 percent to adequately represent the general LGBT population. Organizations with no trans board members in 2008 included GLSEN, HRC, Lambda Legal, NCLR, and PFLAG.

Why is this so? There are many reasons. The first is that attracting a straight transgender person to support an LGBT organization requires the same effort as attracting a straight non-transgender person. But their support can be just as powerful too.

Some of the transgender people who are gay remain leery of LGBT organizations. They remember how transgender people led the charge at Stonewall, only to be forced aside by a gay rights movement wanting to present a mainstream image. They remember how some gay and lesbian people hijacked the Brandon Teena and Barry Winchell murders as gay hate crimes when they were actually hate crimes against transgender people. And they remember how the Human Rights Campaign (HRC), the country's largest LGBT organization, maintained for several years that including transgender people in a proposed Employment Non-Discrimination Act (ENDA) would diminish its chances of passing.

Most LGBT organizations now wish to be transgender-inclusive. If my experiences on the boards of Point Foundation, GLAD (the LGBT legal rights organization unrelated to GLAAD) and Fenway Health are any indication, that transgender-inclusion wish is truly sincere. In fact, those organizations would gladly add other transgender people to their boards if only they could find others who were willing and qualified.

But getting more transgender people on LGBT boards is not easy. Most organizations require board members to be active fundraisers for the organization. Some even have a set annual dollar amount that the board member must contribute personally or entice others to give. This is more of a challenge for transgender people, who are more likely to be underemployed or unemployed because they face even greater discrimination than gay and lesbian people. Moreover, the friends of a transgender person are likely to be other transgender people who face similar discrimination.

Transgender people wishing to undergo medical treatment or physical transition have even fewer disposable dollars because insurance generally does not cover transgender health care. On the other hand, those who do have adequate resources are more likely to pass well in their perceived gender, making them better able to deny being transgender in order to avoid the related stigma. For them, serving on an LGBT board would mean outing themselves.

Some LGBT boards make an exception to the fundraising requirement when a candidate has strong expertise in a specific area such as strategic planning, law, finance, organization development, or human resources. Still, the candidate's own financial situation must be stable enough to permit a focus on the needs of the organization.

It's clearly not enough to have just one of us on an LGBT board. Donna Rose and I have been the sole transgender members of the respective LGBT boards we have served on; Donna was even on the HRC board for a while. We both lament the difficulty in adequately representing all of those under the transgender umbrella whose experiences differ from ours, including drag queens, drag kings, intersex, and genderqueer people.

What is it that board members do, and why does the lack of transgender people on boards matter? Generally, they define, oversee, and advance the mission of the organization and serve as ambassadors to the world on its behalf. They ensure that the organization has adequate resources to carry out its mission and that those resources are adequately protected. They hire, support, and review the chief officer of the organization. Pretty important stuff: all the more reason to have a transgender person on the board.

For transgender people who are too shy to participate in in-your-face activism, being a member of an LGBT board is a great way to support transgender rights. It affords a chance to work with some of the LGBT community's most successful and best-connected leaders. And it gives the transgender community a voice in an organization that has significantly more resources (and sometimes greater influence) than trans-only organizations.

The only downside of being a transgender person on an LGBT board may be that one has to continually educate fellow board members about what it means to be transgender, just like we have to do for the rest of the population.

MY STORY

22. How I Got Started Writing

On February 11, 2006 I buried my wife of thirty years. A sad day, for sure, but also a remarkable one. Remarkable because Barbara and I had lovingly stayed together in spite of my transition from male to female in 2002. And especially remarkable because those last few years before her death were some of our best.

I've been told that only 20 percent of married couples survive the transition of a spouse from one sex to another. Some do so for the kids but in the absence of any real relationship. Some stay friends but without intimacy. Yet Barbara and I had it all!

That's little comfort to me today—I miss her so.

I have always been attracted to and been more comfortable being around women. When I was seven, I used to get together with the neighborhood girls and try on their clothes. When my parents learned of this, they made it abundantly clear that what I was doing was terribly wrong. I don't fault them for that—they were just being good, responsible parents of the 1950s. But their admonishment was so clear that it sent me into a period of heavy denial that did not end until the late 1990s when I first saw another transgender woman and realized I was not alone.

Soon after reaching the point in 2002 where I could no longer live as a male, I started pondering what transition would mean for my sexual orientation. It didn't take long to figure out that I still liked women, regardless. That discovery led to one of my more embarrassing moments when I said to Barbara, "I've got great news. I'm a lesbian!" I was positively excited because I thought this fact would allow us to stay together. But my excitement evaporated in a flash when Barbara replied without hesitation, "Well, I've got bad news, dear. I'm not!"

But Barbara worked hard to understand. Imagine my emotions on Valentine's Day, only a few weeks after I had told her of my plans to transition from male to female, when she sent me roses! I'm so glad Barbara gave it a try because along the way she discovered that she did not want to be any less loving with me in my changed anatomy.

An Associated Press article referred to the groundbreaking 2005 movie *Transamerica* as "more of a healing family comedy than a threatening exploration of transgender issues." I had a chance in early spring 2006 to watch the movie with some friends from my church. (To my knowledge, I'm the only transgender member of the congregation). Afterward, over dinner, I answered one question after another about the movie, about being transgender, and about me and my late wife. I guess that was the "threatening exploration" part. Yet it struck me that the friends were curious, not threatened. They had never had anyone else around to talk to about this stuff.

It's a familiar story for me. It started when I joined the board of directors of GLAD (a Boston-based nonprofit organization that focuses on litigating cases to advance

LGBT equality). GLAD's lawyers had already scored several victories for transgender rights, but there had never been a transgender presence on the board. As GLAD's first trans board member, I was surprised at how welcome I felt and, more importantly, how anxious everyone was to learn more. When I became the first transgender member of the board of Point Foundation, an organization that had already given scholarships to transgender students, I felt warmly welcomed again. I continue to feel welcome elsewhere.

All of this goodwill had me believing that there is a lot of healthy curiosity and interest in understanding transgenderism—and few easy ways to do so short of going to the library. So in 2006 and 2007, I wrote a series of columns designed to cover all of those questions that people are afraid to ask and to do so in bite-size chunks. Those columns were first published on Advocate.com, and I have since updated them to form the basis of this book. I hope that, like Barbara, you'll stay with me (to read the entire book, that is).

23. Mutual Transformation: My Return to My All-Male College

I didn't think I would ever return to the Hanover Plain. It's not that I didn't have fond memories of my time as an undergraduate: learning probability and statistics from Professor Kemeny, discovering just how useful a time-shared computer could be, and getting up in the wee hours to do the morning newscasts for the college radio station, to name a few. It's just that I had some uncomfortable memories too.

Mine was the last all-male undergraduate class in Dartmouth's history; my name was Jeff back then. During my freshman year, the only women undergraduates on campus were visitors. Everything changed sophomore year with the admission of the first freshmen women as well as the female transfer students for my class. By the end of sophomore year, I was tired of—and embarrassed by—all of the shenanigans the men were playing on the women around campus and needed a change of perspective.

So, while some chose to study abroad their junior year, I chose to attend Smith College on the Twelve College Exchange. Guys joked that I was going to "study a broad," given that I was to be one of forty-five men among 2200 women, but that really was not how I felt. I steadfastly stuck with my change of perspective line.

At Smith, I was surprised how much more comfortable I felt among all those women, and I seemed to be a better student because of it. Along the way I met Barbara Wermeyer (Smith '75), and we were married the weekend before my Dartmouth graduation.

I loved living with Barbara but remained strangely embarrassed by things that most guys are proud of. It wasn't until 1995 that I first encountered others who shared my gender questioning and realized I was not alone. I started reading everything in sight, but it wasn't until early 2002 that it became obvious that my true gender was female.

If that sounds precipitous, it really wasn't. I first knew something was amiss when I was age seven. I played more often with the neighborhood girls than the boys. When my parents learned I was also trying on the girls' clothes, they made it abundantly clear that was not something a "good" boy did. I don't fault them for that—they were just being good, responsible parents of the 1950s—but their punishment sent me into a period of intense denial.

I might have transitioned sooner to live as a female had there been greater public awareness of transgender people. There was no shortage of stereotypes and Hollywood images during my life, but none of them ever seemed to fit me. It wasn't until I read *Crossing*, the autobiography of noted economist and university professor Deirdre McCloskey, a transgender woman, that I realized that transgender people came from all walks of life. I was not alone.

At first Barbara was not sure how she would feel about me after my sex reassignment surgery. I was heartbroken and yet not surprised. I had been told that most couples do not survive a spouse's gender transition. But Barbara felt reluctant to throw away the twenty-seven years we had enjoyed up until then. She decided to give it a try. I'm so happy that she did because the years that followed my surgery in 2003 were some of the happiest of our thirty years together.

I did my best to blend into society as a woman. Without the years of socialization that most women have, I was lucky to have the patient guidance and advice of Barbara.

Soon after I transitioned, I learned of the second Dartmouth Gay, Lesbian, Bisexual, and Transgender Alumni Association (D-GALA) reunion for students of all classes. Second? Somehow I had missed the first one. Regardless, I was intrigued.

I'll never forget the day Barbara and I set foot on the Hanover Green for the first time in thirty years. My heart was pounding. But my fear could not have been more misplaced. I found that my alma matter had been transformed! I was welcomed and even embraced by students, faculty, staff, alumni, and their guests. What followed was a euphoric weekend filled with incredibly relevant panels and presentations and great social events. Barbara and I left Hanover positively eager to return again.

And we did—for my own class's reunion in the summer of 2005. Everyone I spoke with was at least cordial, and a few made a point of expressing their genuine happiness that I came back. One classmate explained our class's newfound openness this way: "Most of us are parents now, and we've heard it all."

I returned again in October of 2005 to speak about transgender awareness at the invitation of the office of institutional diversity and equity. It was yet another wonderful weekend in Hanover, one year after my first return to campus.

My positive experiences actually got me wondering what it would be like to move to Hanover to work for the College. Imagine my dismay when I learned that Dartmouth did not include gender identity and expression in its nondiscrimination policy. Fortunately there's good news on that front: in June 2006 the trustees rectified this situation, making Dartmouth the seventh Ivy League institution to do so. I am so proud of my alma mater for this.

The college marked this momentous advance at the D-GALA breakfast during the 2006 Reunion Weekend. In front of the fifty or so people assembled, President Jim Wright reiterated his desire to have Dartmouth "be a whole community, with its richness coming from the diversity of perspectives and ambitions of all its members." And with those words he awarded me a replacement class of 1975 diploma, showing my name as Joanne instead of Jeff. I was in tears.

It was also a bittersweet moment. Barbara—the love of my life, my companion for my reconnection to Dartmouth, and the woman who truly loved me "'til death do us part"— had passed away just a few months earlier after a long battle with cancer. I'm certain that one of the many reasons she hung on so long was to be sure that I got safely established in my new life as Joanne. She was an amazing woman in so many ways.

So now I am a widow and single for the first time since my teenage male years at Dartmouth. As I adjust, though, I can take some comfort in knowing that I have reunited with my Dartmouth family. And who knows? Maybe some day I really will come to work for the college!

24. My Faith Story

My late wife Barbara and I had both been raised in the United Church of Christ (UCC) tradition by our families but had not been members of any church in our thirty years of marriage. When she started losing her battle with carcinoid cancer in the spring of 2005, however, we felt we could not transit the time remaining without a stronger spiritual connection.

Yet, as a transgender woman, I wondered if any church would accept me. There were lots of stories circulating in the transgender community of parishioners in various denominations who had been cast out of their congregations upon disclosing their transgender status. Regardless, I felt I needed to try.

In looking around the web for a UCC church near us, I quickly came upon Old South Church in Boston. Old South had been welcoming lesbians and gay men for quite a while, which I took as a good sign since I usually found myself welcome in similar places. Still, Old South's "Note on the Inclusive Dimensions of God's Grace" did not specifically mention gender identity and expression. We decided to give it a try anyway even though other transgender people might have given up at this point.

We were in tears during much of our first service at Old South ; it was strongly meaningful in so many ways. Could we become regulars? I needed to confirm that I would be welcome.

In the following week I met with Associate Minister Jennifer Mills-Knutsen. She said that Old South's statement including individuals of "every sexual identity" was meant to include transgender folks, too. She cautioned me, though, that I might be the first one of "me" in the congregation!

So Barbara and I became Old South regulars, and we loved not only the church and the service but also its people. No one seemed fazed by two women who were so clearly a couple, and we felt even more welcoming energy toward us as my transgender status came to the fore.

In October of 2005, we became members. I was surprised at how emotional I became to hear Senior Minister Nancy Taylor pronounce my name from the pulpit. It was a recognition of my new name and true gender in the eyes of God and by all of the members of the congregation. How wonderfully reaffirming!

Barbara's last time in Old South was the day she became a member. From then until her passing in January of 2006, the congregation provided extraordinary support for the two of us as her health failed her, and they continue to watch over me as I adjust to my new existence as a widow.

Shortly after Barbara's death, Old South's annual report was published. Imagine my surprise when Rev. Taylor called out as one of the highlights of 2005 Old South's welcoming of its first transgender member of the congregation!

Yet, one question remained in my mind. Would another transgender person feel welcome when the "Note on the Inclusive Dimensions of God's Grace" did not clearly say so? In November 2007, Old South's Board of Deacons invited me to attend their meeting to tell my story and present my proposal that the note be updated to reflect current terminology. The Deacons unanimously accepted my proposal, and in January 2008 the Church Council voted to clarify the note to include "every ... gender identity and gender expression."

All of my doubts about being welcome in a house of God are now gone for good.

Here is how Old South's updated Note on the Inclusive Dimensions of God's Grace now reads:

> Old South Church in Boston, in the name of its host, Jesus Christ, and in the spirit of Christ's invitation carved into the stone of this church's portico, "Behold I Set Before You an Open Door," welcomes all who seek to know God.

> Following the One who we believe is Sovereign and Savior, we affirm that each individual is a child of God, and recognize that we are called to be like one body with many members, seeking with others of every race, ethnicity, creed, class, age, gender, marital status, physical or mental ability, sexual orientation, gender identity, and gender expression to journey together toward the promised realm of God.

We invite everyone to join in the common life and mission of our reconciling community through participation and leadership in this congregation, and by fully sharing in the worship, rites and sacraments of this church.

As we all move forward with the work of this church, we commit ourselves to making justice and inclusivity a reality in this congregation and in the world. On the threshold of Christ's open door, we rely upon the healing, unconditional nature of God's love and grace to be our help and guide.

25. Reflections on Five Years in My New Life

October 2007 marked the fifth anniversary of my transition to living as a female and more profoundly, the twelfth anniversary of encountering other transgender people for the first time and realizing I was not alone in my gender questioning for all of the years leading up to that moment.

Transgender people often use the term "transition" to mean the specific point in time when one starts living in the gender opposite the one assigned at birth. Historically, treatment standards, as well as the need to be highly closeted about your new gender presentation to avoid discrimination, have forced us to make this change appear as instantaneous as possible.

But my experience has been that transitioning genders is a process that continues for years in increasingly subtle ways. It's a profound change, and there is just no way to know going in exactly what lies ahead. If you truly understand that living in another gender is way more complicated than wearing different clothes, chances are that you will be prepared to deal with, and even appreciate, the aspects of life that will be uniquely different.

Take something as mundane as a urine test. It was two years after my transition and one year after my sex reassignment surgery when my doctor handed me a cup for the first sample in my new life. I remember staring at him blankly and thinking, "How does this work now?" Gosh, it sure was a lot easier in my prior life. Don't worry; I did figure it out and laughed doing it. It's a small price to pay for living an authentic life.

A more profound surprise was my initial relationship with the tampon disposal box in the ladies' room. On more than one occasion I found myself staring at it with tears streaming down my face. It's a whole part of womanhood that I missed and that I would have happily endured if I could have been born with a female body. Don't worry here, either. After having enough non-trans women laugh at me for this emotionality, I'm now at peace with that box.

I had never considered that my transition might come up in the death of loved ones. After my mom passed away in 2004, a friend called my dad shortly after to say, "The paper screwed up the obituary—they say you have a daughter." I was proud of my dad for stepping up and telling his friend about my change. But I was also incredibly sad that my dad had to deal with any aspect of my transition at that moment when the focus should have been on my mom.

When my wife Barbara passed away in 2006, my sister-in-law offered to assemble photo collages of Barbara's life for the memorial service. Until that moment I had steadfastly resisted showing anyone pictures of the former male me. Folks who knew me in my prior life sometimes refer to me as "he" even today. But Barbara married a guy, and it would have looked silly to cut me out of the pictures from our wedding, so a lot of people got to see Jeff for the first time. Again, a small price to pay for living an authentic life.

It wasn't until after I had decided to transition that I realized that my sexual orientation was not going to change. I was clearly still attracted to women. That led to one of my more embarrassing moments when I said to Barbara, "I've got good news—I'm a lesbian!" I figured that fact would justify us staying together as a same-sex couple, which I very much wanted to do. Of course, she put a quick end to my excitement when she said "I've got bad news—I'm not."

But Barbara did lovingly stay with me in spite of my transition. And while Barbara was alive, it didn't matter how bad the anti-gay, anti-trans news was during the day; I still came home to someone who loved me unconditionally. I was surprised by how much that love allowed me to be comfortable being out as transgender, way more out than I had ever imagined.

Although my sexual orientation never changed, I essentially became a lesbian when I transitioned. But I had gone into my new life with a partner, and so I had never experienced the lesbian dating scene as a result. I then found myself going through a second coming out—as a lesbian this time. I knew the dating drill from the straight side of things, but who takes the initiative when there is no guy in the equation?

I was surprised at my brother's reaction to that development. "I thought you said you were going to assimilate" as just another woman, he reiterated. I told him that I was doing exactly that by being in social spaces where other lesbians hang out, trans or not. Somehow I don't think that was the kind of assimilation he meant.

Barbara's health was my focus in her final years, so after she passed away I found myself with free time on my hands and in need of occasional breaks from grieving. One day I spontaneously went bowling, my first time since high school. I had a blast.

Now, when you are a casual bowler, bowling is just a party sport. Oh sure, "extreme bowling" exists, but it does not involve skateboarding to the foul line to throw the ball. It does involve black lights, loud music, and videos—extreme *party* bowling, really.

But when you bowl a lot and are somewhat good at it, bowling becomes a nerdy sport. I started going more often, and by summer I was bowling in a league. I was definitely hooked. The surprise here has been that, after overcoming the stigma of being trans, it has been a piece of cake to overcome the stigma of loving to bowl.

My transition seems to be continuing in ever-more subtle ways, and as Martha Stewart would say, "it's a good thing."

26. On Family Acceptance

When a person transitions from one gender to another, the person's family must transition too. That has certainly been the case for mine, although I have been extremely lucky that my family has done more than most to adjust to my new existence.

As I related in my last chapter, transgender people tend to use the term transition as if it were a moment in time, but my experience has been that transitioning genders is a process that continues for years in increasingly subtle ways.

It will likely take longer before my family feels that the changes are subtle. I'm going to share some of my family's transition challenges because I suspect they are shared by others. You rarely see these challenges written about and awareness of them before I transitioned would have helped my family and me immensely.

1. Lingering hard feelings because I imposed my transition

In preparing for transition in 2002, I read up as much as I could to prepare myself. Memoirs and Web sites of transgender people have traditionally painted a picture of rejection by friends, family, and colleagues, and so I announced my transition to my family as a foregone conclusion, determined to move ahead regardless of the obstacles they might put in the way. I knew I was female and was hell-bent on getting to the right gender.

My family was understandably upset and hurt to have had no say in the process.

What I know now is that those stories I read to prepare for transition were heavily skewed toward the negative, combative side of things. Transgender people who have had good transition experiences have generally been too busy in their new lives to share their stories.

I have heard since my transition of one friend who asked her family to help her pick her new name and of another who asked her parents, "What name would you have called me if I had been born a girl?" In hindsight, gestures such as this little one might have gone a long way toward including my family in the process. Of course, my family might never have gotten to the point where they encouraged me to transition, and I doubt I would have ever decided not to transition. But at least they would have known that I do value their opinion and care about their feelings.

2. My broken promise that I would "be the same person"

Before I transitioned, I promised that all that would change was my name, gender, and appearance. I realize now what a foolish promise that was. I was transitioning to get away from a life I did not like! Of course I was going to be different in much more complex ways.

In my case, I have found incredible happiness in my new life and comfort in being Joanne. I don't want to hide anymore. I want to have friends and be with people. I am more open to trying new things and less worried about failing at them. In short, I am far from the person I used to be. While this may be great for me, I need to keep in mind that, for my family, it has meant getting to know a relative they never knew they had.

3.   My broken promise that I would blend in and not be a poster child for the movement

Before I transitioned, I told my family that my goal after transition was to get to the other side and live as just another woman without ever mentioning my transgender status. Treatment standards used to label anyone who could not blend in a failure, and many still work hard to blend in as a result. I did not want to embarrass my family by having the stigma associated with being transgender.

Yet I found most aspects of my new life so much better than my old that I went to the people who had helped me through transition to thank them. Each person responded, "Don't thank me, pass it on to the person coming behind you."

At first I was not sure how to do this. But after the umpteenth friend/colleague said, "Gee, I never understood transgenderism until you explained it," I decided I would be an educator on the subject. After all, if my family and I had known more before my transition, wouldn't things have been easier for us?

Educating people required being visible, first in sessions with small groups and ultimately taking me to regional television and a national magazine. Each step out was nerve-wracking. But each effort was incredibly well-received and appreciated, thereby encouraging me to do more. I now am certain that there is a force larger than me constantly pushing me beyond my personal comfort zone to educate as many people as possible.

My promise to my family to blend in was unreasonable. And while my accomplishments in public can be exhilarating for me, my family needs to know that there is more to me than being transgender. They need to hear about the rest of my life and know that there are still things we have in common.

4. My seeming desire to invalidate the past

I am lucky that I am usually recognized as a female when I am out and about. Yet with people who knew me before, or people who learned about my past before we first met, there is a disquieting tendency for them to call me "he" in spite of my female appearance. This is as non-flattering for me as it is for any other woman, transgender or not.

For that reason, I don't show pictures of the old me, and I resist talking about my life before transition. My old life was uncomfortable. I did my best to get along based upon my understanding of what society expected of men, rather than an innate sense of being male. Along the way, I acquired a reputation as a perfectionist because I was so unsure that I was measuring up as a male.

Today, I find myself less concerned about perfection and much more willing to be me, warts and all. I let my innate sense of being female be my guide.

But my family still has pictures of the old me on display in their homes (as well as of the new me, of course). It turns out that they liked Jeff. Well, I certainly didn't! But the fact of the matter is that I had lots of good times with my family as Jeff, and without those good times I would have been downright depressed. Acting as if my life started when I transitioned, which in many ways is true for me, can seem to invalidate those good times and even the entire time we spent together before transition. It is therefore important that I allow Jeff to be in the conversation with them.

5. My sudden dislike for technology

I was a bit of a technology geek in my old life and my family tended to depend on me to set up computers and fix problems for them. It's clear now that I used technology as a way to avoid interactions with people. Computers don't care about your gender, so working with them gave me time away from the stress of acting male since being male was not innate for me.

After transition, I quickly came to resist and resent technology because it kept me away from people. I was so comfortable in my new life that being with humans seemed much more interesting and desirable.

My shift away from technology was perhaps the most visible sign to my family that I was no longer the same person. But there is hope here. Technology is now aggressively advancing personal communication, meaning it is now a way for me to have more interactions (not less) with people. I've slowly been letting technology back into my life.

6. My socializing with others who are like me instead of those who knew me before

I had few friends in my old life. Most of them were actually corporate colleagues and business associates of my late wife Barbara. My life was consumed with work. I had few hobbies and did little outside of work with the exception of my taking French lessons. While Barbara's friends have generally been accepting of my transition, Barbara is no longer around to bridge the gap between their experiences in the corporate world and mine in the nonprofit world, and so we have tended to drift apart.

In my new life I am outgoing, social, and have lots of new friends. Friends are now so important to me that I find it hard to believe that I had few before. My new friends are disproportionately in the LGBT community because it remains challenging to be gay in the world, and it's much harder to let one's hair down when that is an issue.

But my new social life can easily give my family the impression that I have no contact with the non-LGBT world, which is far from true. I need be sure I also mention my interactions with my colleagues at work, members of the congregation at church, and now my fiancée's large extended family.

7.   My being gay

I have always been attracted to women and that did not change when I transitioned to live as a female. I was lucky Barbara was willing to try staying with the new me after my transition, even though she was quick to insist that doing so did not make her a lesbian. As Barbara was dying of cancer, she would frequently encourage me to find someone else after she passed away. That's just the type of caring person she was. But finding someone else was the last thing on my mind even months after her January 2006 passing. I felt more blessed than most to have had thirty years with such a wonderful woman.

It was only when I realized that I might possibly live for another thirty years that I decided I would prefer to live those years with someone else. And I didn't even think twice; I knew that person would be female. It took me some time to learn how women meet women (it turns out the technology called online dating is very helpful for this), and by 2008 I was dating Terry. As you find out in the next story, Terry and I are engaged to be married in 2010.

I never wavered in my attraction to women. I transitioned in 2002 and knew I was gay then. Yet my family did not think of me as gay until I started dating women in 2007. And when Terry and I got engaged in 2009, they found themselves further challenged by their views on gay marriage. I may think the major activities of my transition are complete, but for them the major activities are still very much underway. I need to be sensitive to this in my interactions with them as we go forward.

So my family is continuing to get to know the relative they never knew they had. It's going to take a while longer, but I'm going to keep working at it. I love them and so I want to keep them in my life, and I want them to keep me in theirs, too.

27. I'm Engaged!

It should have been a strike. My ball in the eighth frame hit right in the pocket, yet the seven pin stayed standing. I turned toward the ball return to get my ball for the second roll, and there was Terry on her knees, holding a ring! "Joanne Herman, would you give me the honor of spending the rest of your life with me in wedded bliss?" I shouted "*Yes*!" and all of the women of the Wednesday night Top of the House women's league erupted in applause as Terry and I shared the warmest of all hugs.

I can't believe how lucky I am. I have found another wonderful and caring woman who loves me as much as I love her. She is so comfortable and such fun to be with. Even better, Terry has chosen me based solely on knowing me as Joanne yet fully aware that I am a transgender woman. I truly must be in heaven!

It seems like fate. In my case, it took almost eighteen months for me to get up the nerve to put myself on Match. com. It wasn't that I wasn't ready. It was because I did not know whether or not to disclose my transgender status. Trans people generally believe that disclosure will almost certainly result in no dates.

But I was so out as a transgender woman at that point that I assumed any date would quickly figure it out when they googled me after I had given them my name. It was after my niece put things in perspective for me that I made a New Year's resolution to go for full disclosure. I posted the following profile on Match.com on January 1, 2008:

> I was widowed in early 2006 and am therefore single for the first time in thirty years. Fortunately I'm fairly self-sufficient, meaning that life is still active and interesting on my own. Still, I miss the spontaneity and variety that a partner adds. I know my next partner will not be like my first, and I'm excited, not sad, about that prospect.
>
> I do think I'd prefer someone who is a Meyers Briggs Type Indicator 'I' like me (I'm an INFP). I may have a fairly public life, but at the end of the day I'm exhausted and need to recharge.
>
> I love my job for so many reasons, not the least of which is because of it allows me to be active outside of work (I am on the boards of a few social justice organizations) and leaves my weekends free. Others might describe me as kind, caring, loving, loyal, sensitive, responsible, conscientious, and worldly.
>
> Keeping trim is fairly important to me, although I do that more with diet and activity than with exercise. That's a good thing because I do love to dine out, although dining out is way more fun with a partner.
>
> I never had children and probably would not want to bring them into the world at this

point, but I have love enough for yours if they'll let me into their lives.

I don't know how to be any way other than honest in life, so I feel I need to tell you something up front—I love to bowl. I go bowling at least once a week and am reasonably good at it. Embarrassing, isn't it?

If you can accept that fact about me, then you'll probably also be able to accept the fact that I am a post-surgery (2003) male-to-female transgender woman. My teenage niece tells me, "Anyone who rejects you solely for the reason that you are transgender is not worth your valuable time and effort." She's been right about so many other things that I have to trust her on this.

If you are still reading, that means you are likely fairly confident about your place in the world, and I like that. If you are also sensitive, independent, and smart, we should talk.

It turns out that Theresa (Terry) Fallon had just listed herself on Match.com too. Terry had held back for years out of concern that an electronic dating service would be too impersonal. Yet she was anxious to get on with the next chapter in her life after raising two daughters as a single mom, so her sisters succeeded in convincing her to give it a try.

When she found my profile and read the transgender part, she found herself thinking, "Wow, what incredible honesty. Just what I am looking for." And when she saw that I love to bowl, she blurted out, *"Yes!"* because she does too.

Terry e-mailed me right away, and we had our first date on January 13 of last year. After a coffee that turned into a three-hour lunch, we each knew that we had found someone very special. We started e-mailing daily, then chatting daily, then seeing each other more and more until it no longer made sense to live apart. She moved in with me in May of 2008.

I helped her move out of the home where she had raised her daughters, she nursed me through the recovery from my retinal reattachment surgery, and we even bought a new set of living room furniture together. All were good tests of any relationship, and we passed with hardly a squabble. Each day just seems to get better and better.

So now, more than a year after we first met, we are anxiously planning our wedding and excitedly looking forward to a long life together. And I have the overwhelming sense that my life is about to be complete, because now I will be the bride I always wanted to be.

RESOURCES

28. Ten Books I Recommend

When I figured out in 2002 that I was transgender, I started reading every book available on the subject. While I have a pretty good handle on my own situation at this point, I'm still reading. Here are my current favorites:

1. On whether transgender individuals are really mentally ill:

Gender Madness in American Psychiatry: Essays From the Struggle for Dignity (BookSurge, 2009) by Kelley Winters, PhD Could it be that: 1) The diagnoses that label trans people as mentally ill are based largely upon the opinion of a handful of psychiatrists imposing their view of what is socially acceptable behavior? 2) These psychiatrists base their opinion almost entirely on studies of their own patients without considering the large number of transgender people leading well-adjusted lives who don't feel the need to see a psychiatrist? 3) These psychiatrists are suspiciously relentless in challenging the credibility of anyone who seeks to challenge their opinion? 4) Their opinion ignores significant studies by other professionals showing that most individuals who transition genders have positive outcomes? 5) The diagnoses are written in a way that remove the mental illness label for a patient who undergoes reparative therapy (which claims to make an individual not trans) but not for a patient who transitions genders, even if the outcome is positive? And 6) Some of these same psychiatrists happen to specialize in reparative therapy and therefore have a vested interest in labeling trans people as mentally ill?

You'll be hard-pressed to see these statements as anything but true after reading Winters's painstakingly researched book. Winters documents how the *DSM IV* diagnoses of the American Psychiatric Association came to be and why reform is needed. She carefully shows that the diagnoses are based more upon variance from societal norms than distress or impairment caused by gender dysphoria, thereby labeling all gender non-conforming individuals as mentally ill—even those not experiencing distress.

Winters demonstrates how this official word of the APA is then used to justify job terminations, lack of insurance coverage, and other types of discrimination. Even the HRC Corporate Equality Index, which aims in part to end transgender discrimination in the workplace, inadvertently causes it according to Winters. The CEI allows a corporation to score 100 percent by offering mental health counseling as its only transgender health benefit, and corporations overwhelmingly chose this benefit over four others, Winters asserts, because the *DSM IV* recommends reparative therapy for those who seek counseling.

Gender Madness is a must read for those concerned that some of the psychiatrists who helped develop the *DSM IV* diagnoses and who have a vested interest in maintaining them, have lead roles in the development of the *DSM V* to be released in 2012.

2.   On transgender children:

The Transgender Child: A Handbook for Families and Professionals (Cleis, 2008) by Stephanie Brill and Rachel Pepper. The psychiatric community tells many parents of transgender or gender non-conforming children that reparative therapy is what their children need. After the therapy fails and makes their children even more miserable in the process, or for parents who decline to go that route in the first place, there is now hope. The handbook is a compassionate resource that includes tips on how to deal with the social, psychological, educational, medical, and legal consequences of accepting a child as transgender or gender non-conforming. The book includes a foreword by the leading expert in the United States on the care of transgender youth, Dr. Norman Spack of the Gender Management Service clinic of Children's Hospital Boston.

3.   On how sexism makes things more difficult for those who transition to female:

Whipping Girl: A Transsexual Woman on Sexism and the Scapegoating of Femininity (Seal, 2007) by Julia Serano. Male-to-female transsexuals like me are the women who give up male privilege for femininity. Serano shows how much this fact threatens the patriarchy and how transition treatment standards (set largely by men) have tended to objectify and pathologize us. If you believe the psychiatrists who say we transition just to wear pantyhose, you should buy this book to read the real reason. If you feel it is just that transsexual women are excluded from such venues as the Michigan Womyn's Music Festival, you should buy this book for a convincing explanation of why such policies are flawed from the feminist point of view. If your thinking has been formed by the feminists who've vilified us over the years, none of whom are transsexual, you owe it to yourself to buy this book to hear our side of the story.

4. On the importance of being out and visible:

Becoming a Visible Man (Vanderbilt University, 2004) by Jamison Green. Green is a great writer, and his memoir does a fabulous job of chronicling his transition from female to male. What I most appreciated and took to heart, however, was his stress on the importance of being visible as a transgender person. He convinced me that my trans visibility working inside an organization can be just as powerful as someone else's trans protest signs outside the building. After all, the protester's message can have more impact when someone like me is on the inside to explain it. My life has not been the same since I read this book.

5. On transgender legal rights:

Transgender Rights (University of Minnesota, 2006) by Paisley Currah, Richard M. Juang, and Shannon Price Minter. Short essays by some of the leaders in transgender activism and academia, collected by three of its most prominent members. This book examines recent and current laws and their application, the gains achieved during this same period, and the political actions taken or needed. A must read for those in the developing field of transgender law.

6. On transgender history:

Transgender History (Seal Studies, 2008) by Susan Stryker is a deep dive into American transgender history from the mid-twentieth century through today. As an LGBT historian, Stryker provides proof that transgender people are not a new phenomenon but rather a minority whose progress has been limited from years of being pushed aside by the gay rights movement. A must read for those pushing for transgender rights legislation.

7. On what it means to trans:

The Riddle of Gender (Anchor, 2006) by Deborah Rudacille. Rudacille, who is not transgender, is the science writer at Johns Hopkins University. While lots of things not helpful to trans people have come from JHU, this is a shining exception. Rudacille combines extensive research and conversations with prominent representatives of the trans community to give us a comprehensive overview of trans history, science, and activism in an easy-to-read form. As Publishers Weekly put it, "Lively enough to be a good introduction for the educated lay reader and documented enough for the scholar."

8. On understanding transsexualism:

True Selves: Understanding Transsexualism—For Families, Friends, Coworkers, and Helping Professionals (Jossey-Bass, 1996), by Mildred L. Brown and Chloe Ann Rounsley. Written by clinical therapists, *True Selves* is a useful introduction for those just starting to identify as transsexual as well as for their immediate family and others with a strong interest or concern. Written in an easy-to-read and compassionate manner, the book dispels misconceptions about transsexualism and provides useful suggestions for the hurdles people may encounter in the process of transitioning. This book is a classic, and there is nothing else quite like it. But as transgender understanding continues to advance, the text will soon need an update.

9. A transgender story—non-fiction:

She's Not There: A Life in Two Genders (Broadway, 2003) by Jennifer Finney Boylan. A successful travel writer and popular Colby College English professor, Boylan tells the story of her life and her gender transition. Boylan's spouse stayed with her through her transition, as mine did, and

Boylan does a good job of giving voice to her spouse and her spouse's emotions throughout the process, something not found in most transgender memoirs.

10. A transgender story—fiction:

Trans-sister Radio (Harmony, 2000) by Chris Bohjalian is an engaging and wonderfully-written story about a man and a woman who fall seriously in love before gender transition, then choose to continue the relationship after the male character transitions to female. Bohjalian is not transgender but seems well-informed since most of the plot is accurately reflective of the trans experience. *Trans-sister Radio* has been quite popular, having been subsequently made available in audio CD, cassette, and download.

29. Tips for Talking With a Transgender or Gender Non-Conforming Person

1. If the person's gender presentation is unclear or inconsistent, use the person's first name instead of the pronouns he and she.

2. Don't ask what the person's prior name was.

3. Don't ask what the person's current name means (this is true for other minority groups, too).

4. Don't make comments about appearance that would be offensive to a gender-conforming person.

5. Be aware that the person may not identify as gay. Gender identity and expression is not the same thing as sexual orientation:

    *   Sexual orientation means who one loves;

    *   Gender expression means how one looks and acts;

    *   Gender identity means how one lives one's life.

6. When speaking with someone who identifies as genderqueer:

    - Accept that the person may feel genderless or partially male and partially female;

    - Understand that the person may feel totally comfortable being genderqueer and may have no plans become fully male or female;

    - Realize that the person may list sexual orientation as "queer" because "gay" and "straight" are not applicable.

7. When speaking with someone who has undergone a gender transition:

    - Remember that sexual orientation is based on current gender: a male-to-female trans woman dating a man is therefore *straight*.

8. Don't ask about surgery or hormones:

    - Very few gender non-conforming people use hormones or undergo surgery;

    - If the person discusses surgery or hormones, you may ask about the person's well-being but not about details of the procedures.

9. Be careful with the words you use:

    - Say "transgender" not "transgendered" (after all, you say "gay," not "gayed");

    - Say "transgender person" (adjective) not "a transgender" or "a trans" or "a sex change";

- Don't ever use hermaphrodite, she-male, tranny, transvestite.

If you find yourself in a situation where classification is desired (applications, etc.)

1. First, ask yourself, "Is classification really necessary or just gratuitous?"

2. If you must classify, suggested choices for sexual orientation:

    - Straight

    - Questioning

    - Gay

    - Lesbian

    - Bisexual

    - Queer

    - Pansexual (means: loving all without regard to sex or gender)

3. If you must classify, suggested choices for gender identity (select no more than two):

    - Female

    - Male

    - Cross-dresser

    - Gender Non-Conforming

    - Transgender F-M

- Transgender M-F

- Other (please elaborate)

Caveat: Terminology is constantly evolving. These tips should be updated regularly, preferably with the help of someone currently of undergraduate college age.

30. Web Resources

Children, resources for parents of: abcnews.go.com/2020/story?id=3089992&page=1

Corporate Equality Index: www.hrc.org/cei

GLAD Transgender Rights Project: www.glad.org/work/initiatives/c/transgender-rights-project

Media Reference Guide: www.glaad.org/Document.Doc?id=25

No-Match Letters: nctequality.org/Resources/NoMatch_employees.pdf

Peeing in Peace: transgenderlawcenter.org/pdf/PIP%20Resource%20Guide.pdf

Prevalence: ai.eecs.umich.edu/people/conway/TS/Prevalence/Reports/Prevalence%20of%20Transsexualism.pdf

Real ID final regulations: www.nctequality.org/PDFs/RealID_March2008.pdf

Religious literacy quiz by Stephen Prothero: http://www.beliefnet.com/section/quiz/index.asp?sectionID=10002&surveyID=428 or http://www.chron.com/channel/houstonbelief/religiousiq/

Remembering Our Dead: www.gender.org/remember/about/core.html

Reparative therapy: ai.eecs.umich.edu/people/conway/TS/News/Drop%20the%20Barbie.htm

Standards of Care: www.wpath.org/publications_standards.cfm

Transgender Day of Remembrance: www.transgenderdor.org

Index

Index

About the Author

After almost half a century living as a male, Joanne Herman transitioned in 2002 to live as a female in order to resolve a gender incongruity she had felt for as long as she remembers. She has since been active as a spokeswoman for transgender awareness and understanding.

Joanne's numerous columns written for Advocate.com, a popular LGBT news Web site, have helped educate readers about transgender and gender non-conforming people and the issues they face. They are the foundation for this book.

Joanne is the first transgender person ever elected the Boards of Directors of Fenway Health, the largest LGBT-focused health center in the world; Point Foundation, the national LGBT scholarship fund; and GLAD, the New England LGBT legal rights organization. She retired from the GLAD Board in 2009 to devote her time to GLAD's Transgender Rights Project and remains fully active on the Fenway and Point Boards.

Joanne is the first openly transgender member of the congregation of Old South Church in Boston (United Church of Christ), the same church where Benjamin Franklin was baptized and Samuel Adams served as a deacon.

Joanne is one of the first openly transgender alumnae of Dartmouth College, and a graduate of the last all-male class. Dartmouth's President James Wright awarded her a Class of 1975 diploma in her new name in 2006.

In 1975, when her name was Jeff, Joanne married Barbara Wermeyer (Smith '75) at the Smith College chapel. After Joanne underwent sex-reassignment surgery in 2003, Barbara willingly stayed with Joanne. Barbara helped Joanne get established in her new life while Joanne helped Barbara battle a rare form of cancer known as carcinoid. Joanne was widowed from Barbara in 2006 after thirty years of marriage.

Joanne holds a BA in Government and Economics from Dartmouth and an MS/MBA from Northeastern University. She is currently Financial Controller at New England Foundation for the Arts and lives in Boston with her fiancée, Theresa (Terry) Fallon. Joanne is also fluent in French and an avid bowler.